I0223637

Happy (Freilich) Days Revisited:
Growing Up Jewish
in Ike's America

Happy (Freilich) Days Revisited:
Growing Up Jewish
in Ike's America

Compiled and Edited by
Jack Nusan Porter, Ph.D.

Contributions by
Jack Nusan ("Jackie") Porter
Gerald S. ("Gerry") Glazer
Sanford L. ("Sandy") Aronin

Copyright © 2010 by Jack Nusan Porter and The Spencer Press
ISBN: 978-0-932270-39-9
ISBN: 0-932270-39-5
All rights reserved. No portion of this book may be copied, reproduced or transmitted in any form without prior permission from the publisher.

Published by The Spencer Press
79 Walnut Street, Unit 4
Newtonville, Mass. 02460-1331
jacknusan@earthlink.net

Cover Photo: Gerry Glazer at his wedding; Sandy Aronin is peeking out second from left.

Acknowledgements
All photos and ephemera are the property of each author except where noted. In particular, the photos of the Milwaukee Fruit Peddlers Association are from the Milwaukee Jewish Museum and are used by permission.

Jack Porter acknowledges the help of Howard Karsh, Sheldon Bankier, his brother Reb Shlomo Porter, sister Bella Porter-Smith, and Jay Hyland. Plus, Robert Smyth for designing this book and Todd Larson for typing it.

DEDICATION

From Jack Porter:
I dedicate this book to my dear mother
"Momma Feygeh" Porter-Arenzon
who passed away
at age 100 on December 1, 2009

From Gerry Glazer:
In memory of
Dorothy Glazer (1914-2007)

From Sandy Aronin:
In Memory of father & mother
Jacob and Sadie Aronin (Epstein)
&
grandfather & grandmother
Samuel and Leah Aronin

TABLE OF CONTENTS

INTRODUCTION

It was a real pleasure writing and collecting these memoirs. These are three memoirs of the old West Side in Milwaukee in the 1950s. Unlike the original "Happy Days" shown on TV, these memories show the clash and ultimate reconciliation between a secular and an Orthodox or religious (*frum* in Yiddish) orientation, a perspective never shown on TV. However, my memoir is different from the other two. Plus, Gerry and Sandy are older than I am. (In July of 2010, I was 65 and they were two and eight years older than me, respectively.)

I went through many transformations. I started out *frum* but then became more of a "conservative" Jew and then later a "Labor Zionist" Jew, then a "radical" Jew, and then a "post-modern, non-denominational" Jew."

Gerry and Sandy have not; they have remained *frum* Jews, but with a tolerance and respect for others that comes from growing up in the Midwest, especially in such a *menschleich* town as Milwaukee and its north-west side.

Also, I will deal with such topics as dating and sexuality in a separate memoir because I felt it was inappropriate in this particular book. Other memoirs will include my coming to America, the more secular side of growing up in the '50s, my Israeli memoirs of 1962-1963, my radical 1960s memoirs, my years in graduate school at Northwestern University, my years in Boston, my time as a rabbi in the late 1990s, my Key West interlude in 2001, and my years since then.

I might add that Gerry's parents finally moved to the Milwaukee Jewish Home and the shul, Beth Jehudah, moved from 54th and Center into a remodeled shul on 52nd and Burleigh, and has thrived in its new location. Life goes on. Change goes on.

The key influence in their memoirs is that of the late Rabbi Jacob Twerski and his family, especially his wife Leah and their sons Michel (and wife Feige), the late Motel, Shea, Aaron, and the late Shlomo Twerski. However, the influences on my religious life were more complex and diverse — Labor (Socialist) Zionism, Yiddish, Conservative Judaism, and later political radicalism, the New Left and the Counterculture of the 1960s.

My parents belonged to a conservative *shul,* but then moved up the street to the Orthodox Congregation Beth Jehudah, but they were always tolerant of all branches of Judaism from secular Yiddish culture to Labor Zionism to Modern Orthodoxy.

Originally, journalist Andy Muchin and I were to write a history of the Jews of Milwaukee, but then sadly Andy's teenage son died suddenly, my wife passed away, and we were in no mood to write such a complex book. Instead, Andy went on to do outreach into the Jewish communities of the South, and I went on to other projects, three in particular: first, this memoir of the old West Side; second, a booklet examining the relationship between Hollywood and Milwaukee; and third, the full memoirs of my entire life. It should keep me busy.

Happily, an excellent author, John Gurda, was chosen by the Milwaukee Jewish Federation to write a long-overdue history, building upon the famous Switchkow-Gartner book of fifty years ago.

My acknowledgments to Gerry Glazer for his fine editing skills and his photos, for correcting some serious errors, for suggesting the title, and for his unstinting support over this decade and a half; to Sandy Aronin for his contributions, his photos, and his unflagging good humor and wit; to Howard Karsh for his knowledge of the Sherman Park area; to Jay Hyland of the Milwaukee Jewish Museum for his help with pictures and other material; to Kathy Bernstein and John Gurda for their support; and to all the wonderful people of the old West Side for their memories.

I hope that others will write their own memoirs and submit them to me. For example, I tried but could not find a female or a non-Jewish African-American or Catholic voice.

In any case, thank you and I hope to hear from you.

Jack Nusan Porter
jacknusan@earthlink.net
(617) 965-8388
July 20, 2010

JACKIE'S STORY

by
Jack Nusan ("Jackie") Porter

The old West Side of Milwaukee was an area that
was bounded by North Avenue on the south, Capi-
tal Drive on the north, 60th Street on the west, and
Sherman Boulevard on the east. Today it is called
Sherman Park and is about 70% African-American. A
small pocket of Orthodox Jews live north of Burleigh
from about 48th Street to 60th Street, including the
Roosevelt Drive area.

The only person I know (though there may be other
Jews) who live south of Burleigh today is one of the
authors, Gerry Glazer. I used to live in a green and
brown duplex at 2912 North 50th Street at 50th and
Locust, and Gerry and his wife Cissy live just up the
street at 2944 North 50th Street.

I go there often whenever I'm in the old neighborhood and sometimes I even get a chance to go into
my old house. The present tenants are a lovely black
woman and her daughter, and the house, both inside

and out, looks better today than it did when we lived in it from 1954 to 1996, when my mom, Feigeh Porter, moved out due to increased crime and old age. It is eerie to see the basement, the attic, the garage, and the tiny postage-stamp back yard that held our *sukkah* (shed). Who today goes back to their old home? That's how powerful an impact it had on me.

The neighborhood I remember is vastly different today than it was in the '50s and '60s. It was more diverse, more secular, safer, more vibrant. I miss it. My parents, Irv and Faye Porter, came from Europe to America in July 1946 as survivors of the Holocaust. They arrived in Ellis Island on the Marine Perch, a recommissioned U.S. Army vessel with literally nothing in their pockets except some old photos. After a brief stay in New York City, they moved to Chicago to live with an uncle and aunt of mine, Morris and Betty Porter and their son Allen, in the old Rogers Park area near Lake Michigan. (Ironically, this area is still one of many immigrants, and my cousin Allen, age 81, lives a mile north in Evanston, Illinois.)

I remember nothing from that period. A year later, in 1947, we moved to Milwaukee, since jobs and housing were scarce in Chicago, plus we had many cous-

Cute little Jackie, age 2, June 15, 1947, already with books to read and study.

6

ins — the Kliegers and the Liebermans — up there who could "sponsor" us refugees from Europe by helping us with jobs and housing.

We found such housing in a dilapidated section of Milwaukee at 2125A North 10th Street, between Garfield and Lloyd, just south of North Avenue. Today, our house is in the center of the I-43 Expressway. They tore up and destroyed my neighborhood for "urban renewal," tore down all the housing and built new urban subdivisions — actually, I must admit, quite nice ones. They look just like homes in suburbia but are in the inner city, close to the expressway and downtown. No more ugly "projects." I have even seen some whites there. But if you look hard, you can still see some of the old alleys and garages where the horses were stabled ("Tomatoes! Potatoes!" old Mr. Cohen would yell while driving his horse and cart through these alleys).

Before global warming. The big snow storm of winter 1947, sitting on the street with my proud dad Irving Porter in front of our house on 10th Street. Mr. Cox's BBQ and custard store is in the background.

Jews had long moved out of that area, to the East and West Sides, when we moved to 10th Street, and then would move again as Blacks became dominant. But we were just poor refugees, and we stayed in that "ghetto," today called the "Inner Core." It had been a thriving Jewish center in the 1920s and 1930s, especially around Walnut Street, but by the time we got there in the late '40s, it was transitioning. Most Jews had moved out. Only us *greeneh* ("greenhorns," slang for European refugees) lived there, and we dreamed of moving on out as soon as possible.

Yet institutions remained. *Shteiblach* ("religious houses" in Yiddish) of rabbis, like Grand Rabbi Jacob Twerski were in the area (located at 11th and North). The old Beth Medrash Hagodol *shul* was also there. There were still some kosher meat shops, occupational and fraternal groups had their social clubs, such as the OKUV building on North Avenue, and the scrap metal and fruit/vegetable cart sellers association all had their meeting places, but soon they would all be gone.

However, the largest remaining institution was an Orthodox *shul* named Beth Israel

Three fast friends sitting on a log in winter 1950 in our dilapidated neighborhood, in the back yard of 10th St . . . . From left, Shelly Bankier, Jackie Porter, and Solly Porter.

(it became Conservative in 1957). Located on Teutonia Avenue, one block west of 13th Street, just over a block north of North Avenue, it drew hundreds of people to its annual High Holy Day services in the fall. It had a choir led by Chazzan (Cantor) Moses Sorenson, and the rabbi was the respected Harold Baumrind.

I remember going to the basement of that *shul* even after we moved out in 1953 (to 50ᵗʰ and Locust on the West Side) for High Holy Day rehearsals. My brother Sol, our friend Benny Lande, Mr. Smotkin, and several others comprised the all-male choir. No women voices were allowed. Hazzan Sorenson had a power-

Recess at the old Hebrew Academy on Teutonia Ave., circa 1952. In back from left, Michael Marks, Carl Coopersmith, Freddy Geller, and Shaul Baumrind (the rabbi's son); in front, from left, Allan Rabinoff, Joey Blasberg, Shelly Bankier, and Jackie Porter. Troublemakers all, looking so very prim.

ful personality and a magnificent voice, and people came from all over the city to hear us "perform." I can still remember the poignant and mysterious Nesaneh Tokef service: *"Utifiach tov...ma vee'erim"* ("Who shall live and who shall die in the year to come, we pray you, Lord, save us, help us… to live and not die").

It was a huge *shul,* and I am happy to say that decades later I was instrumental in making it into a national historical site with its beautiful glazed windows and neo-Moorish design. Today it is the Greater Galilee Baptist Church, and little has changed inside since the 1940s.

However, the major influence in my young life was attending the old Milwaukee Hebrew Academy in the basement of that *shul.* We entered through the back entrance, opposite the playground. You can still see it today. The stairs seemed awfully big back then, since we were so much smaller. I went there for three years from 1950 to 1953, from ages 5 to 8, and the friends I made there — Sheldon (Shelly) Bankier, Arnie and Harry Peltz, Carl Coopersmith, Freddie Geller, Michael Marx, and the rabbi's son Shaul Baumrind — became lifelong friends.

Even the teachers — Rabbi Manfred Pick, Rabbi Harold Wininger, Rabbi Hillel Horowitz, Mr. Springer, Mrs. Evelyn Raskin — have stayed in my mind forever. In fact, it was, despite what some have claimed, the very first all-day Hebrew school in Milwaukee. Initiated by a community-wide coalition of rabbis such as Rabbi Jacob Twerski, Rabbi David Shapiro, Rabbi Harold Baumrind and including lay people such as Sol Blankstein and Mrs. Geller, it was a demanding schedule of English classes in the morning and Hebrew classes in the afternoon. Gym was running around on the playground.

Teachers were tough. If you didn't behave, you were rapped on the knuckles with a stick. If you swore, you were taken down to the basement and your mouth was washed out with soap! We were wild kids, and I remember running away from school at age six or seven because I was angry with a teacher. I got lost, and wonderful Mrs. Bertha Wolf, the large jovial cook, saw me and took me <u>home</u>, not back to school! That's how close a community we were.

My mother was shocked when she got home, and I don't know if I was punished or not. Maybe I was. My Dad had a long "strap" (belt), and he used it on me. I remember running under the bed, my dad lashing the strap out trying to hit me before my mom came in and rescued me. "Talk to the child," she used to implore him. Today, they call it "child abuse"; back then, it was simply a parent's right to discipline their kids. Times have changed.

I ran with a "black gang." My closest friend was Michael, a wiry, curly-headed, good-looking guy, somewhat like a younger version of Michael Jackson, but a bit older than me. He showed me all the good hiding places, the barns where the horses were kept, the alleys, the small parks where we could hide. I had no prejudice. I still don't. I was what Norman Mailer called a "white negro," an outsider-insider, running with black boys and knowing no racial difference or prejudice until much later. A kind of bourgeois Eminem, so to speak. I can still do a mean imitation of hip-hop with a Yiddish accent to this day. Back then it was called "playing the dozens."

It was an idyllic time. But then we moved to the West Side, to a nicer house and a nicer neighborhood, a house with a broad green lawn, my own bedroom, and new schools.

Instead of working in a factory that made him break the Sabbath laws, my dad went into business with a German Jew named Sigmund Singer. They bought some trucks and with Singer's contacts in the German, Slavic and Polish communities, gathered scrap metal and sold it to larger, usually Jewish firms like Afram Brothers, Bass Brothers, Balco Metals, and Miller Compressing. My father and Siggy had a falling out, and my dad set up his own scrap metal business with a black truck driver ironically called Elvis Tarkington. My mother was always a homemaker, but she took in paying "boarders" to make ends meet.

Soon, my brother Sol was born at Mt. Sinai Hospital in November 1947, followed by my sister Bella, born at St. Joseph's Hospital in November 1954. We went to a "conservadox" (traditional Conservative) *shul,* Beth Medrash Hagodol that had

My bar mitzvah at Beth Am center, December 21, 1957. From left, my proud mom Faye Porter, my brother Sol, me, and my Dad carrying my sister Bella. Look at that huge Cake.

also moved to the West Side, to 50th and Center, and led by Rabbi Greenman. I was *bar-mitzvahed* there under him in December 1957. (I recited the Chanukah *"Roni V'simchi" haftarah,* Prophet section.) But after Greenman left, Temple Menorah, its new name, became Conservative under Rabbi Isaac Lerer, and my parents left to go to Twerski's *shul* up Center Street.

I had a lovely *bar mitzvah* party at Beth Am Center. I even have pictures of it. Cantor Sorenson sang. My brother Sol (now called Shlomo) has a funny story of that time. It seems that the cantor wore dentures, and one time, when he hit a high note, his dentures popped out, to our utter amusement. Sadly, my folks ran out of money and did not have enough for a lavish

At my bar mitzvah, my friend's table. From left, Howie Loeb, Rosalyn Pais, Al Saxe, Shelly Bankier, Willi Rosman, and Ralphie Felder.

13

bar mitzvah for Sol. He had to make do with a smaller home party. Sorry, Sol.

After Sol went to a *yeshiva* in Skokie, Illinois, in September 1962, with Benny Lande, my parents became more religious. Sol did study the *Shulchan Aruch* and some *Talmud* with Rabbi Michel Twerski in preparation for the Skokie *yeshiva*.

However, my greatest influences were not from *frum* rabbis like Rabbi Twerski, but from a secular Yiddish-based Hebrew school called the United Hebrew School on 55th and Burleigh and from the *Ichud Habonim* Labor Zionist Youth Movement. Thus, Yiddish and Hebrew culture merged together, and, along with my experiences at secular schools such as Sherman Elementary School on 51st and Locust, Steuben Junior High School on 51st and North Avenue, and Washington High School at 2525 North Sherman Boulevard (Sherman and Center), I developed a complex mixture of philosophies and outlooks.

This, plus the rising tide of "teen culture," would all form the strange and fascinating combination of influences that affect me today and make up Jackie Porter.

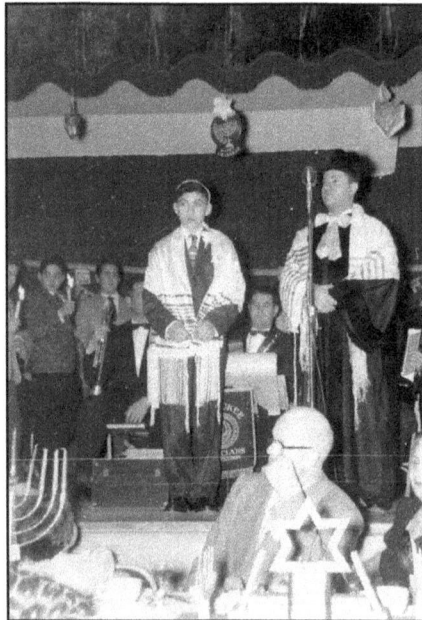

My Bar Mitzvah, December 21, 1957
with Cantor Sorenson on my left, the big band
behind, and Avrum Lerer and Ida Sonin in front.

Replacing the all-day Hebrew Academy on Teutonia Avenue was a twice-a-week-plus Saturday morning Hebrew school at the old Beth Am ("House of the People" in Hebrew) on 55th and Burleigh, a single story, low, flat, reddish-orange brick building with no basement and no second floor.

We learned in rooms named after Labor Zionist leaders such as Golda Meir or other secular leaders like Max Kamesar. The school had a definite Zionist slant, and also housed the local *Ichud Habonim* youth group in which I was an active member, rising to be *"Rosh Ken,"* president of the local chapter. We stressed love of Israel, cooperative living, *kibbutz* values of sharing, progressive socialist politics, and Israeli singing and dancing. *Habonim* had its own summer camp and winter conferences. It was lots of fun. It concluded with a yearlong trip to Jerusalem and Kibbutz Gesher Haziv in 1962-1963 (which will be described in a separate memoir).

The old Hebrew Academy had folded in 1954 for mysterious reasons. My brother, now Reb Shlomo Porter, thinks that it simply ran out of money. Others think that a rabbi absconded with the money and ran off to Canada. But maybe they were just a bit ahead of their time, not yet having a firm financial base, which was about a half-decade into the future. Its successor, the Hillel Academy, was founded in 1960 by Leo Guttman, and my sister Bella attended that, as well as an all-girls' high school in Chicago in the late '60s.

But for me it was Beth Am Center with its eclectic menagerie of students from a wide array of backgrounds. Our only competition was Mr. Garfinkle's

"New Method" Hebrew school on Center Street, operating out of a storefront, plus the growing number
of synagogue Hebrew schools.

Looking back at the Beth Am Center, it was in a way
a fine example of community-wide Jewish education,
similar to the Solomon Schechter schools of today but
with a much more solid influence of Yiddish and then,
later, Hebrew and Israeli-related courses and clubs.
Milwaukee had a long Zionist tradition going back to
the 1920s and with Golda Meir, a strong Labor (read:
Socialist) Zionist community. Important families like
the Melroods, the Lutzkys, the Barlands, and others
stood out.

*The famous Khuli photo of our graduation class of 1957 from the United Hebrew Schools
on the West Side, a classic picture. Bottom Row, seated left to right: Norman Cohn,
Chanita Stillerman, Dalia Golan, Rosalyn Pais (Mr. Pais's daughter), Varda
Schwartzman, and John Gilman. Top Row, left to right: Mr. Mordechai Melrood
(Hebrew teacher), Jackie Porter (dig that hair!), Sheldon Bankier, Fred Geller, Mr.
Morris Schwartzman, (Hebrew teacher and Varda's father), Al Teplinsky, Lennie
Weingrod, Mr. Kniaz (singing teacher), Barry Ellman, Howie Loeb, Alan Saxe, and
Mr. Herman Pais (Hebrew teacher).*

I still remember the Yiddish theatrical troupes of Ben Bonus and Mina Bern (husband and wife), who came in from New York in the '50s and '60s to that small stage at Beth Am for their annual performances. I remember our annual Habonim cantatas, given around Passover, directed by the beautiful Yiddish actress Bess Lerner, that combined dance, song, and spoken word. I remember the Friday evening *Onegei Shabbat* with its white paper tablecloths and little cups of wine. Our youth leaders were Harry and Lorna Kniaz (who later moved to Madison), Assaf Alterman, our Israeli *shaliach,* and Ilana Berner, today running a bed-and-breakfast in Caesarea. Wonderful, wonderful

Members of the Milwaukee Fruit Peddlers Union (later, scrap metal and paper union) gathered for a meeting in the late 1940s. Irving Porter is in the middle row, second from left, with the colorful tie and balding head. Others include Abe Chudnow (top row, far left); Isadore Petterman, Nat Goldberg, and Sam Eichenbaum (top row, fifth, sixth, and seventh from left); Louis Schumacher (middle row, third from left); Max Chudnow (seated, far left); Rubin Atinsky (middle row, second from right); Louis Rudack (seated, second from right); and Harry Siegel (seated, far right). Photograph courtesy of Mary Kramsky Atinsky and the Milwaukee Jewish Historical society.)

17

teachers and role models, all of them.

Our Hebrew teachers were for the most part secular Hebraists, not *frum,* bur perhaps coming from *frum* families. I call them the Hart, Schaffner and Marx of Jewish teaching, and they all had a profound impact on me. First, there was the aging and strict *Mar* (Mr.) Morris Schwartzman, a brilliant teacher with absolutely no patience for youngsters. His two daughters, Varda and Hasia (ancient Biblical names), were also in the classes, and I remember one time, my friend Shelly Bankier being thrown out of class for laughing at something that Varda did. Hasia Schwartzman Diner went on to become a well-known Jewish historian at New York University, and Varda became a lawyer and health executive living in the Washington, DC area. They were both active in Milwaukee *Habonim* and at its summer camp as well.

Then there was the gentle and refined Mr. Herman Pais, also the father of two daughters. Pais led the Saturday morning services. It was from him that I learned the beautiful melodies of the reader's repetition of the *Amidah.* He was a wonderful man, and I miss him terribly. He had patience with kids.

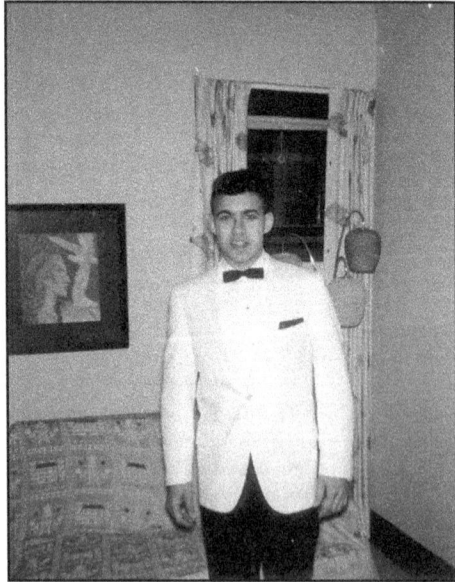

My June 1962 prom photo

18

And kind of in-between, both gentle and tough, was Mr. Melrood, the grandfather of Laurie and Elise Melrood, both active *Habonim* people, the father of Paul Melrood, an important Jewish and Zionist communal leader, and the father-in-law of Mrs. Melrood, also a dynamic communal leader. Mr. Melrood was a good Hebrew teacher.

We also had Mr. Kniaz, a one-legged teacher of Yiddish and Hebrew songs taught on Sunday mornings, accompanied by an excellent accordion player. To this day, I don't know how he lost his leg — was it the war in Europe or the Pacific, or maybe due to diabetes? He had a wooden leg which he took off at times and was the butt of many pranks, like hiding his wooden leg. Boy, was he mad.

At Sol's bris, Mt Sinai Hospital, November 1947, with assorted cousins—Kleigers, Liebermans, Kaufmans, Magidsons, Sokols, Schoenfelds, and Kaplans. My dad in his nice hat stands in the center, second row. To his left is "Uncle" Hershel Kleiger. To his right, Lou Kaplan and Lottie Magidson; To her left is Sophie Kaplan; above her is Inez (Schnooksie) Schoenfeld. Minnie Klieger is above my dad; David Kaufman is also to my dad's left; Rose Kaufman is also there. Some husbands like Arthur Magidson and Harry Schoenfeld are missing, as is my mother, naturally; she is upstairs after giving birth to Sol. In the rear, left to right, Sammy Hornik, Larry Weidenbaum, and Morrie Hornik.

I still remember gong from *shul* to *shul* on the High Holy Days. I would start at Beth Jehudah at 54th and Center and then go to Adudas Achim at 58th and Burleigh, sometimes stopping off to throw a few basketballs in Sherman School Playground at 51st and Locust. Shelly Bankier, my brother Sol, and I would meet up with Harry and Arnie Peltz, Joey Blasberg, Arvin Peltz, their cousin, and others. Sometimes there were girls too, like the Galina twins, Karen Kashakow, and others. We even got some *davening* in.

What was especially moving was that during *Yizkor,* the time of remembrance of the dead, especially *Shoah* dead, all of us who had living parents would have to leave the *shul* and go outside.

We knew we were getting older when we had lost a parent and had to stay for the *Yizkor* service. Most of us thankfully had both parents.

There is more to be said, but I will say more in my own memoir. What happened was that the Jewish community moved from the near North, the old Walnut Street area, today known as the "Inner Core" or "Bronzeville", when it became African-American, to the West Side, today known as the Sherman Park Neighborhood. No neighborhood exists forever. They all change, some slower than others, but eventually no Jews lived in the Walnut Street area, and the once-vibrant Jewish community of the West Side gave way to a more integrated, diverse community.

The Jews, as usual, moved on, when crime and color changed. Those *freilich* days are gone, gone forever, except in our memories.

Our new home on 2912 North 50th street

Mom and Dad at the Milwaukee airport in the 1970s

Shlomo, my brother, in the ally behind our house were we played.

*A visit from my uncle and aunt from Los Angeles---Morris (Morrie)
and Betty Porter (top right) with my folks (top left), me (bottom right
seated), brother Sol, (left), and little Bella above Sol.
In our home on 50th Street, November 1958.*

22

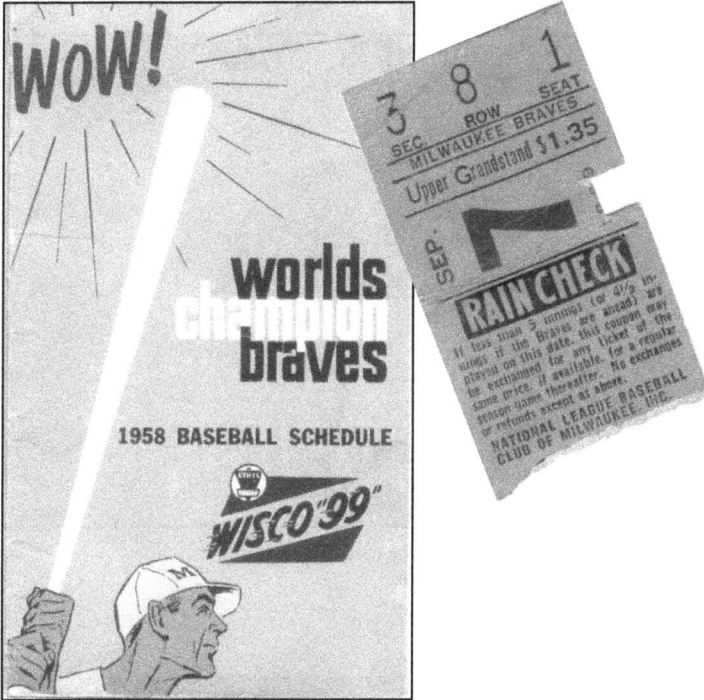

The 1958 Milwaukee Braves baseball team schedule and ticket stub.

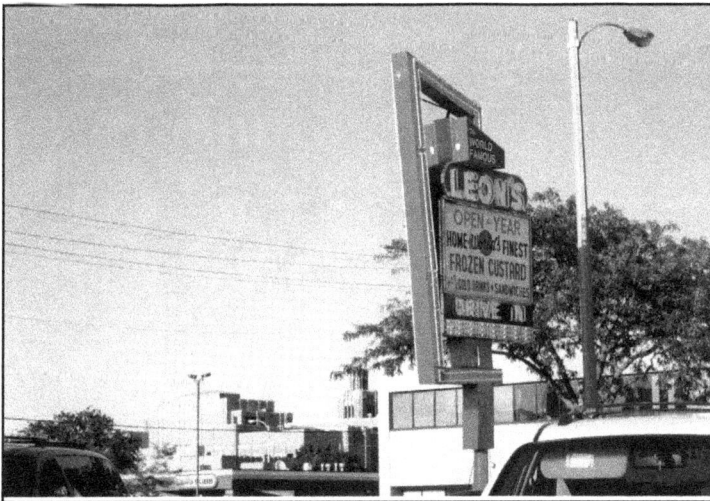

Leon's drive-in on the south side of Milwaukee. Similar to Kopps on the east side and Petroff's on the West side---these were the places where "Happy Days" people hung out. Petroffs no longer exists but the other two are thriving businesses.

Kopp's Sign as it looks today.

Kopp's inside as it looks today.

The dark strange road to Camp Tavor, Habonim - Dror Camp.

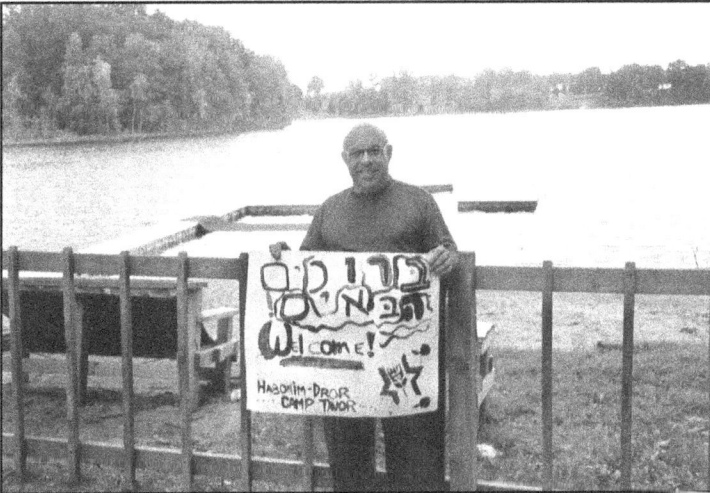

Me holding a sign in front of Kaiser Lake in 2010.

Program for the Milwaukee Pops with Arthur Fiedler conducting.

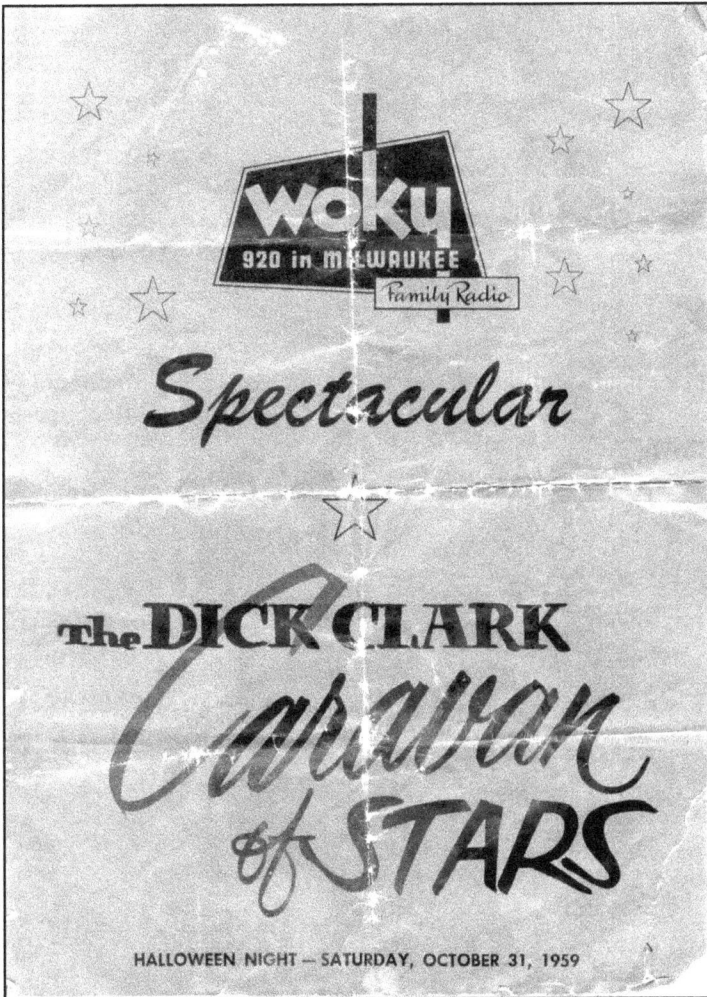

The WOKY 920 AM radio, "The Station of the Stars" promoting "The Dick Clark Caravan of Stars", Halloween night, Saturday, October 31, 1959, with such rock and roll legends as Paul Anka, Duane Eddy, Annette (Funicello), Lloyd Price, Bobby Rydell, La Vern Baker, Jimmy Clanton, Phil Phillips, The Coasters, The Jordan Brothers, and The Drifters---whew! What a line-up!

Me with Reb Michel Twerski at the cemetery, in the 1990s.

The Bobover Rebbe, second from right, surrounded by his Chassidim, New York City, 1990s, at one of his grandchildren's wedding. I took the picture.

*The Rambam <u>machberet</u>, notebook for Hebrew school, dated 1957,
for Mr. Pais's Hebrew class.*

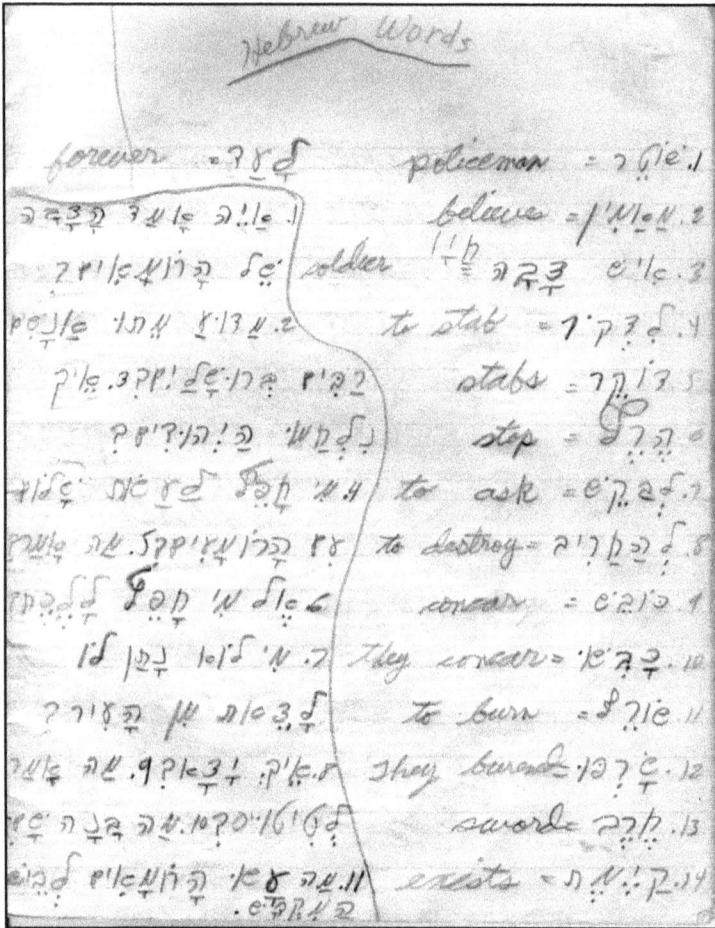

A typical inside page of the <u>machberet</u>, with Hebrew words and phrases.

Jack Porter

הַמַפְטִיר

הִלְכוֹת תְּפִלִּין, סֵדֶר עֲטִיפַת הַטַּלִּית וְהַנָּחַת
הַתְּפִלִּין, שְׁמוֹת הַטְּעָמִים, בִּרְכוֹת הַתּוֹרָה,
פָּרָשִׁיּוֹת הַ"מַפְטִיר" בְּאוֹתִיּוֹת סְתָ"ם וּבְאוֹתִיּוֹת
מְרֻבָּעוֹת, וְהַהַפְטָרָה וּבִרְכוֹתֶיהָ

No. 36

פרשת בהעלותך

שילה

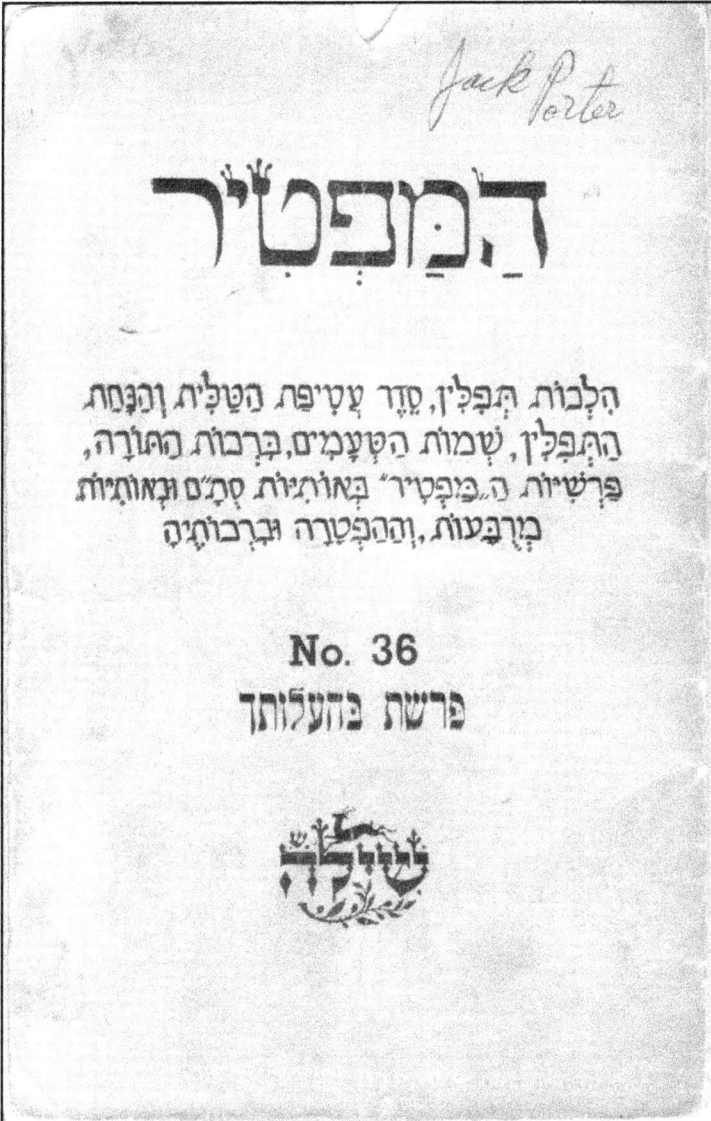

*Finally my ---Maftiv—my bar mitzvah Haftarah, Roni V'simchi, "Sing and rejoice, O
daughter of Zion: for lo, I come, and I will dwell in the midst of thee, saith the Lord" (the
Haftarah of Beha-alotecha, Zechariah II, 14-17, III, 1-10, IV. 1-7.*

This is the famous "Partisan Baby" photo, taken by Soviet photographers, in Rovno, Ukraine, January 1945, after liberation by Russian troops, with me on the laps of my mom, Feige Merin Puchtik (Porter), age 36, and my dad, an honored partisan commander, age 39. Note the leather boots and the "War of the Fatherland, Partisan Medal, First Class" on my dad and the swollen feet of my mom.

Me in Rome at Pope John Paul's Funeral. Yes, In the rain, April 2006.

The old "Beth Am" Center abandoned today.

GERRY'S STORY

by
Gerald S. ("Gerry") Glazer

The Real "Richie Cunningham"

The popular TV series "Happy Days" portrayed a group of fictional Milwaukee teenagers in the 1950s. Since I actually was a male teenager in this city at that time, you might say that I was the real-life "Richie Cunningham," except that Richie was not Jewish. Ironically, the most popular character on the show, Italian-American Arthur Fonzarelli ("The Fonz"), was played by Henry Winkler, who *is* Jewish.

The Ghosts of 16th Street

Today the block of North 16th Street between North Avenue and Lloyd Street in the North Side of Milwaukee looks like it was bombed in a recent war, but never rebuilt. Most of the block is trash-strewn vacant land; the buildings that have survived are old and neglected.

In the middle of this block, on the east side of the
street, stands a brick eight-family apartment house,
the paint peeling from the wood trim. If you follow
the driveway on the northern side of this building to
the rear, you will see a doorway marked 2132A. The
stairway inside leads to two apartments and the basement.

Today the residents of this building are all black, as
is the entire neighborhood. But in 1942 the apartment
on the first floor was the home of Mrs. Ida Joseph, her
daughters Dorothy and Elizabeth, and Dorothy's husband David Glazer.

The building was owned by a Jew then, and about
half the tenants were Jewish too. Just south of the
eight-family stood Feldstein's grocery store, where
Mr. Feldstein would fetch goods with a mechanical

*Gerry's parent's wedding, August 31, 1940. From left to right: Max Joseph (my moth-
er's brother); Hannah Glazer (my father's mother); Dave Glazer (my father's cousin);
Fanny Glazer (my father's sister), my mother and father, Henry Glazer (my father's
cousin); Elizabeth Joseph, Helen Glazer (my father's sister), and Jenny Waldman (my
father's aunt). The flower girl is Shirley Glass, my father's niece.*

hook from the top shelves and the image of a Dutch woman with a broom graced the front door. Past Feldstein's was a duplex, occupied by Mrs. Joseph's stepdaughter Selma Freeman. Beyond that, stood the homes of the Saltzsteins, Jubilerers and Milans.

America was at war in 1942, but David Glazer, though 28 years old, was not in unform. He was spared induction because he worked in a pharmaceutical firm, which was considered essential nonmilitary service. Moreover, Mrs. Glazer was expecting a baby.

On September 26, the second day of Sukkos (Tabernacles), the baby was delivered at Deaconess Hospital by Dr. Frank Margoles, a first cousin of the father. Eight days later, Mordecai Ruby performed the *bris mila* (circumcision) and named the boy Gershon Shabsi, after Gershon Joseph and Shabsi Glazer, the fathers of both parents. The Glazers selected English

The Glazer Family, Summer, 1958

names Gerald and Sherwin for their similarity to the Hebrew ones.

David Glazer was a part-time musician, and enjoyed writing songs. Soon he wrote a lullaby for his baby son that included the following verse:

"Now we call you Gerald,
A name fit for a king,
And soon you'll grow up big and strong
And know everything."

My father never read *Brave New World* by Aldous Huxley, but his lullaby, repeated in my young ears endlessly for years, had the effect Huxley devised for programming the nascent Alphas, who were taught they were to be geniuses.

Before long I learned that America did not have a king, and I had no prospect of becoming one. But the part about someday knowing everything seemed to be a reasonable goal to shoot for. Although my mother did not write songs, nor sing much, she reinforced the idea that I was born to be smart. From my earliest conscious recollection, I have always believed it. (When I became a father, I purposely raised all my children to believe the same thing about themselves, and by all objective measures, it was true.)

My grandmother was a religious woman: she lit candles every Friday evening, attended synagogue services on the holidays, and kept strictly kosher. But none of her three children followed her example. Although I inherited my Jewish identity from my mother, it was my father that raised me as a Jew. When his mother died in 1951, he said *kaddish* at Congregation Beth Israel daily and brought me with him. I did not know any Hebrew at the time, but it was this experience that established my lifelong commitment to *davening* (praying) with a *minyan* (ten men) every day.

I was enrolled in Lloyd Street School, which was already substantially integrated. Students were Jewish, white Christian, and black, but friendships and rivalries crossed all these lines. We kids related to each other as individuals, rather than as members of ethnic groups. I think this experience in integrated schooling has affected my attitude on race ever since: racial difference has simply never meant much to me. The same is true of my father, who attended Ninth Street School in the 1920s. Significantly, my mother first encountered blacks when she moved to Milwaukee from Wisconsin Rapids as an adult, and always viewed them as very alien. Similarly, children educated in Jewish day schools appear to share this attitude today as well.

Gerry at a age eleven

Until fourth grade, all of my teachers were women, mostly of German-American heritage. My first male teacher, Mr. Braun, was interested in science and piqued my interest in the subject. He subsequently became principal of another grade school.

My fifth-grade teacher was Miss Evelyn Margoles, a sister of the Dr. Margoles who had delivered me. Since she was my cousin, I had to learn to address her as "Miss Margoles" at Lloyd even though I could continue to call her "Evelyn" at family affairs. She treated me kindly, but without favoritism.

Our religious life was centered at Beth Israel, a huge Byzantine structure at 2432 North Teutonia Avenue, which is now the Greater Galilee Baptist Church.[1] The main sanctuary consisted of two floors: the lower for men and a balcony for women. To me, the ceiling seemed about a hundred feet above the floor. Weekday services were held in a small chapel in the basement.

The spiritual leader was Rabbi Harold Baumrind, who had performed the marriage of my parents in 1940. As a young boy, I had surmised his name was spelled "Bombrind" and that the name implied that he would "bomb" misbehaving kids out of the synagogue.

The rear of the synagogue was a school. During the school day, this was the home of the Milwaukee Hebrew Academy; after school it became the North Side Talmud Torah.

In the fall of 1952 I was enrolled in the Talmud Torah; my teacher was Abraham Gutnick, whose cousin had been my father's teacher in the 1920s. It was there that I first learned Hebrew and the rudiments of Judaism.

40

Lloyd Street, despite its significant Jewish enrollment, celebrated Christmas every year, with mandato-
ry singing of carols. Once I had begun attending Hebrew School and learned of the struggle of the Mac-
cabees against the Greeks, who attempted to impose
their religion on the Jews, I began to see the parallel
with my own time when Christians sought to make
young Jews like me sing Christian songs in the public
schools. I became an ardent supporter of church-state
separation then, and my political views ever since have
been strongly influenced by my early experience with
religious coercion.

I grew up in a period of rapid change. In 1948 you
could still watch horses pull milk and junk wagons
down our street by day, and watch television at night.
We were the first on our block to have television, and
kids would jam into our small living room after school
to watch the 10-inch Teletone screen. Other children
would watch TV through the windows of appliance
stores, where they missed only the sound. Most programming was local then, and I made my first TV appearance on a talent show for children called "Little
Amateurs." I performed a magic ventriloquism act
which brought rave reviews from the stagehands.

My mother's younger sister Elizabeth was known as
"Liz" in the family. She moved to Los Angeles in the
early 1940s, but moved back a few years later.

Liz was an ardent supporter of Senator Estes Kefau-
ver of Tennessee for the 1952 Democratic presidential
nomination, and she easily persuaded me to follow
suit. I watched the convention in dismay as Adlai
Stevenson won the nomination on the third ballot.

But within a few weeks I got behind Adlai, and was handing out pins and homemade signs for him on 16th Street. I even wrote state Democratic headquarters offering to start a children's Democratic club and sent a poem to the Milwaukee Journal about the election, which became my first publication. I was deeply disappointed when Dwight Eisenhower won, especially that he carried Wisconsin. Still, Stevenson carried the City of Milwaukee, where I had done all my campaigning, so I didn't do too badly after all, for a ten-year-old.

Sam Glazer, my father's first cousin, was a single man then, as he is now. Having no children of his own, he took a special interest in me. He bought me a *Book of Knowledge,* which I soon devoured cover-to-cover. This book had information about everything from atomic energy to how ice was made and used. I can still picture some pages of it. Sam also took me on field trips to Yerkes Observatory and the Museum of Science and Industry. His influence, together with that of Mr. Braun noted earlier, pointed me in the direction of a career in science.

During this period I also became enamored of ancient Greece, and read translations of Homer's *The Iliad* and *The Odyssey.* Not satisfied with translation, I persuaded my parents to buy me a Greek grammar book and taught myself the language. I can still read Greek, but my vocabulary is very limited. One day I learned that the word "Hellenist" meant a Jew interested in Greek culture, and was surprised to find out that I was not the first one.

Both of my parents became beauticians, and together they opened a shop called the Beauty Centre at

4711 West Center Street in 1946. Within a few years they moved to a better location at 5226 West Center Street. Although working mothers are common today, they were still quite rare in my early years; all of my friends' mothers were home all day. Until my parents came home at night, I was the responsibility of my grandmother.

Ours was a functional family, but one that functioned differently from most others of the time. My mother was the unquestioned leader of the family, and the only one who even tried to argue with her was my grandmother, whose influence was weak and declining. My father, who lost his father when he was four, had been raised by his widowed mother and senior siblings. He had learned to defer to the mother of the household as a boy, and continued to do so as a husband. I, too, adapted to the role of the junior male in a household run by doting women.

We lived in a two-bedroom apartment: one for my parents, the other for my grandmother and Liz (when she was with us). I slept on a cot in the hallway.

In 1952 the Glazers decided to buy a home near their Beauty Centre. A two-bedroom Colonial with den was found at 2675 North 54th Street, just one block west of the shop. With the help of a privately held 4%-interest mortgage, David and Dorothy became homeowners during the first week of December.

On December 8, 1952, the whole family boarded my father's yellow DeSoto; we took one last look at the brick apartment house that had been our home for so long. The car pulled away from the curb and headed north to our new residence on the West Side.

Drawn to the Rebbe's Table

My grandmother's health began to decline during the last months we lived on 16th Street. After the move, she deteriorated rapidly.

The den on the first floor of our new home became her bedroom. A hospital bed was installed, and she seldom left it. Practical nurses were hired to care for her while my mother was at work.

She died on October 10, 1953.

Meanwhile, I continued my fifth-grade education at Sherman School at 51st and Locust streets. My teacher was a wizened spinster named Miss Kunath, who, I learned later, disliked all boys. My adjustment to the new class was difficult, and Miss Kunath treated me with special hostility.

At Sherman, over a third of the students were Jewish and the rest were white Christians. In recognition of the Jewish population, a few insipid Chanukah songs ("Josh Lights a Candle," for example) were included in the fall religious pageant among the usual carols.

The misery of these initial months on the west side was relieved somewhat by making new friends, especially Marshall Berman, a bright Jewish lad from a nonobservant home. I started walking back and forth to school with a girl named Arlyn, and soon we were also going to movies together. She was cute, though chubby, with long brown hair. We dated for about a year, and remained friends long after.

The New Method Hebrew School, where Harry Garfinkel was the owner and sole teacher, was located next door to the Beauty Centre. Although called a Hebrew school, most of the time was spent on learning Yiddish. Like all after-school *Talmud Torahs,* Garfinkel's school prepared boys for their *bar mitzvahs.* But, unlike the North Side *Talmud Torah* and most others, students were not taught Hebrew grammar or vocabulary.

Harry Garfnikel was born in Poland about 1890, and was brought to America during the great migration before World War I. He had attended *yeshiva* (rabbinical school) in Europe, and though never ordained, entered the U.S. Army as a Jewish chaplain. He often noted that the U.S. government had certified him as a "rabbi," but he never used the title. I wondered then what credence should be given such a designation by a non-Jewish government.

Although most Hebrew schools were affiliated with either a synagogue or a Jewish community agency (such as the Board of Jewish Education), Mr. Garfinkel was fiercely independent of all of them. I believe he called his school New Method because he developed his own curriculum and teaching style. His classroom included boys from about 8 through 12 years old; he would teach one group while another did homework. Often the older boys would teach the younger, especially skills such as putting on *t'fillin* (leather-bound boxes of parchment) which was best done one-on-one.

When we moved to 54th Street, my father faced a dilemma regarding my Jewish education. He knew that Mr. Garfinkel would be miffed if I were sent to another Hebrew school. However, he considered it essential that I learn to understand Hebrew, not merely recite it. He offered Mr. Garfinkel a deal: I would be enrolled in New Method if I were given special instruction in Hebrew vocabulary and grammar. The teacher agreed.

Most of the boys in New Method considered Hebrew school a necessary burden to be borne for the sake of *bar mitzvah.* They recited prayers and sections from the Bible without understanding. After *bar mitzvah,* they would leave the school and quickly forget what they had learned. The emphasis on Yiddish was puzzling, since by the 1950s there were few Yiddish speakers to talk to.

Mr. Garfinkel provided several ancillary activities for his students, including a debating club, a Boy Scout troop, and Saturday morning services. I participated in all of them.

After the death of my grandmother, I was home alone a great deal, especially on Saturdays. On the Sabbaths when a Garfinkel student became *bar mitzvah,* no services were held at the school. On these Saturdays my mother suggested that I attend the service at Congregation Beth Jehudah, then located diagonally across from our home at 54th and Center streets.

Beth Jehudah was led by Rabbi Jacob Israel Twerski, known as "The Rebbe." He was born in Hornesteiple, Russia, in 1898, the descendant of a long line of Chassidic rabbis.

Chassidic Judaism was founded in Russia in the 18th century by Rabbi Israel Baal Shem Tov. Chassidism emphasizes the use of song and dance as forms of religious expression, and is closely related to Jewish mysticism. Chassidic rabbis wear long black robes; on the Sabbath and holidays they also wear a cylindrical fur hat called a *shtreimel.* A number of Chassidic dynasties arose in the 19th century; Rabbi Twerski was born into the dynasty of Chernobyl. He married Dvora Leah Halberstam, a daughter of the Bobov dynasty, who became a *rebbetzin,* the Yiddish term for "rabbi's wife."

The Twerskis left Russia after World War I and arrived in Milwaukee about 1928 with their two sons, Shlomo and Motel. Two years later another son was born, named Abraham Joshua (Shea). In 1939, the *Rebbetzin* gave birth to twin boys, Michel and Aaron.

Rabbi Twerski first established his synagogue in part of his home at 11th Street and North Avenue. In 1950 a new structure was built at 54th and Center streets, and the house across the alley behind the synagogue became the Twerskis' home.

When I first attended Beth Jehudah services, Rabbi Twerski was about 55 years old, but seemed much older. Mostly bald and bearing a gray beard, he was attired in his Sabbath outfit of a black robe and fur hat *(shtreimel).*[2] All of his public speeches were in Yiddish, but he knew English well and read both Milwaukee newspapers daily in addition to Yiddish papers and the weekly Wisconsin Jewish Chronicle. Despite his European birth and background, he was well versed in the way of America. He sent all of his sons to college, which was unusual then and remains rare in Chassidic circles today. Local judges often asked him to conciliate Jewish divorces and other disputes. When a Jew got in trouble with the law, Rabbi Twerski would testify for him as a character witness, even if the man had never been a member of Beth Jehudah.

The Rebbe spent most of his days (except Sabbaths and holidays) visiting sick Jews in local hospitals. When I became ill in the summer of 1955, he visited me at home. When he learned that I did not have a Sabbath meal at home on Friday night, he invited me to eat at his home every Friday night, which I did for the next five years. During and after these meals the Rebbe often talked with me about politics, current events, and Garfinkel's Hebrew School.

The Rebbe did not push people into becoming *frum* (orthodox), but accepted them as they were. The Rebbe taught, "Be concerned about the other person's body and your soul, not *your* body and *his* soul!" When he found it necessary to admonish someone, the message was, "You are an intelligent, refined person, so how can you act this way?" He would build the person's self-esteem while showing that his conduct was inconsistent with his true character.

He greeted everyone with warmth and enthusiasm. When asked how he was, the reply was not "Fine," but "Wonderful!", even when he felt far less than that. He liked to play chess, though seldom found time for the game. He rarely lost, since whenever he was at a disadvantage, the pieces would be suddenly knocked over. This became known as the "Twerski defense."

The *Rebbetzin* was an excellent cook. She also read extensively in English as well as Hebrew and Yiddish, and was very knowledgeable about the world beyond the home and synagogue. When visitors were present, she invariably addressed her husband as "Rabbi."

The *Rebbe's* eldest son Shlomo had become a rabbi in Denver years before I first entered Beth Jehudah, but he would visit Milwaukee occasionally and would then address the Congregation. He had brown hair and beard, and deep-set eyes that seemed to pierce anyone he was looking at. He was a brilliant speaker in both Yiddish and English. Unlike his father, he had a distant and somewhat aloof personality, and I never really got to know him. He suffered severe illnesses throughout his adult life, and prayers were often recited for his recovery. (He died of cancer at the age of 58.)

Motel Twerski had a warm and playful personality; he loved riddles and brainteasers. Unlike his elder brother, his eyes were twinkling rather than piercing. Although he was often referred to as Rabbi Motel, he invariably denied having earned the title. He was college-educated as an accountant, but was operating a food store with the synagogue *shamus* (administrator) Aron Richt when I first met him. The store was located in a building directly across Center Street from Beth Jehudah. A fire on Saturday morning, January 11, 1954, destroyed the Twerski-Richt market, which was uninsured. Motel then went to work as an accountant for Sam Bass, the synagogue president who owned a junk and scrap metal business. Motel also worked part-time as a kosher-supervisor at a cheese factory in Oconto, in northern Wisconsin. In December 1957, while en route to Oconto around midnight, his car was struck by another head-on. The other driver was killed instantly, but Motel barely survived. He recovered from his injuries after months of surgery and convalescence. Motel was equally comfortable discussing Torah, science, philosophy or baseball.

Shea, a brilliant student in both high school and *yeshiva,* decided to become a doctor after a few years as the associate rabbi of Beth Jehudah. He was attending Marquette University when I first met him. He was ultra-thin and already had a quickly receding hairline. He had excelled in science, and could deal cogently with apparent conflicts between scientific fact and Torah tradition. Shea was uniquely qualified to bring me around to the Torah perspective, and he always had enough time to answer all my questions and objections. We talked about everything: existence of G-d, truth of the Torah, evolution, Holocaust, Israel, everything. The discussions with Shea in the early months of 1954 led me to a decision to become Orthodox.

The twins, Michel and Aaron, attended Milwaukee Public Schools (Lloyd, Sherman, and Steuben) until ninth grade, when they were sent to the Chicago Yeshiva. The *Yeshiva* was located on Douglas Boulevard, in the heart of Chicago's old West Side, just south of Roosevelt Road. When the Yeshiva was established in the 1920s, the area was solidly Jewish, but became increasingly black after World War II, when most Jews moved further north. *Yeshiva* students often walked the streets in large groups; on the Sabbath their scheduled movements were guarded by police escorts.

One night in 1955 Michel and Aaron were attacked by a group of black youths, who robbed and beat them both. The *Rebbe* then transferred them to the *yeshiva* in Baltimore, which was in a safer neighborhood. (The Chicago Yeshiva moved to Skokie in 1958.)

Michel and Aaron were fraternal twins, differing in height, facial appearance, and personality. Aaron was taller, with a strong angular jaw. His hair was kinky, almost African in texture. Aaron was always assertive, and ready to argue his point of view with vehemence. Michel was shorter, and had a softer appearance, his hair more wavy than kinky. Michel, from his youth, was more introspective and contemplative, and far less likely to raise his voice. If Aaron was "Type A" in modern parlance, Michel was "Type B."

Orthodox boys usually start their *yeshiva* studies at the age of about 14. Since Milwaukee had no *yeshiva,* most local religious boys were sent to the nearest one, in Chicago. Some others went to Baltimore, and some to New York.

However, there were three other boys at Beth Jehudah with whom I became good friends. In order to prevent embarrassment, I am obliged to refer to one of them by a pseudonym.

The most unusual was Sanford ("Sandy") Aronin, whose memoir follows mine. His parents insisted he complete high school before enrolling in *yeshiva,* so he was still in Milwaukee. Since the other religious boys his age were away at *yeshiva,* he associated with guys my age. Sandy was bright, but had an impish attitude. Heavyset and wearing thick glasses, he looked older than his true age, but acted younger. He loved arguments, and often took the "devil's advocate" stance. Sometimes, in the middle of a dispute, he would jump over to the opposite side of the question. In summer he sometimes brought a squirt-gun to the synagogue and used it.

He drew a series of cartoons titled "Enemy of Judaism" on the classroom blackboard of the synagogue, often lampooning people.[3] He wrote a song about me, to the tune of the Hebrew hymn "Yigdal Elokim Chai" with the following chorus:

Oh there is a queer
Who grins from ear to ear,
His hair is in a tangle,
He rattles in high gear.
His voice can 'ere be heard,
He twitters like a bird.
He talks like a 'jack-ankle,'[4]
A fact that can't be cured.

This was the first song written about me since my father's lullaby. Unlike "Now We Call You Gerald," it did not have a lasting impact on my self-image.

I'll call my second friend "Yakov." He was the only boy I knew who was raised in an Orthodox home. He was sharp, and loved pranks and practical jokes.

The third boy was Stanley Martin Schuster, whose Hebrew name was Meir Tzvi. Like me, Stanley grew up on 16th Street, and I had known him briefly when we lived there. Stanley was tall for his age, had wavy brown hair, and wore glasses. Raised in a nonobservant home, he became religious as a result of enrollment in the Beth Jehudah Hebrew School, then taught by Shea. He was shy and inarticulate, and his learning did not come easy. But he made up for all that with a limitless zeal. All the boys at Beth Jehudah learned Torah, but Stanley wanted to learn it every minute. We became best friends, but when Stanley lost interest in discussing or doing anything but learning Torah, we drifted apart.

Once Stanley and I were raising hell in Yakov's first-floor bedroom when he heard his father coming. He quickly opened the window, and Stanley jumped out and left. Then Yakov opened the closet door and ushered me in. When his father opened the door, there was Yakov sitting quietly alone.

"Where's Schuster?" the man inquired.

"He went home," Yakov replied.

"Then where is Glazer?"

"Either he went home or he's in the closet," Yakov said coyly. At this his father opened the closet door.

"Good *Shabbos!*" I greeted him as I strode out, extending my hand to shake his.

Among the older men in the synagogue, I became known for *chutzpah* (nerve). Once an old man notorious for heavy drinking accosted me with the Yiddish phrase "It's time to take a Jewish word into your mouth!"

"It's better than taking *bronfm* [whiskey] into your mouth!" I retorted.

Although I ate at the *Rebbe's* table every Friday night, I was often invited to other homes for Saturday afternoon dinner. Once my host was being kicked under the table by his older son, who was seated between his father and me.

The man picked up a saucer full of meatball sauce and warned him, "If you do that once more, I throw this sweet-and-sour sauce right in your face!" After a few minutes the boy did it again and quickly ducked — guess who received a serving of sauce on his white Sabbath shirt? The lady of the house lent me a shirt to wear home and laundered mine.

Beth Jehudah functioned as our social hall as well as our synagogue. I would bring a chess set to the evening service, and often Sandy, Yakov, Stanley and I would stay late into the night playing chess, learning, or just talking.

One night a visiting *yeshiva* student started to play around with the public address system while Aaron Twerski was reciting his evening prayers alone in the main sanctuary. Turning the volume to maximum, the young man intoned gravely, "This is the Lord, Twerski, and I am not going to accept your prayer!"

Although Marshall's parents were not religious, they did send him to Garfinkel's for bar mitzvah instruction. Ironically, it was he that taught me to put on t'fillin properly. Marshall was a pure rationalist, and found religious beliefs unconvincing. We argued these matters back and forth for years, neither able to change the other. Yet we had much in common: chess, politics, and school life.

Marshall wanted to become a doctor since early boyhood. He had no political preference at that time; he said that if he were to become rich he would be a Republican, otherwise a Democrat.

My bar mitzvah was coming up, and I was determined to make it a memorable one. I prepared to read the entire Torah portion for that Sabbath (a section of Genesis about the birth and youth of the patriarch Jacob) plus the section from the Prophets, and lead most of the prayers. Mr. Garfinkel wrote me a speech in both Hebrew and Yiddish, which I memorized.

I delivered the speech from the lectern of Congregation Beth Jehudah on Saturday morning, November 19, 1955. Rabbi Shea responded on behalf of the synagogue. I was now an adult member of Milwaukee's tiny but growing Orthodox community.

Dissonance

A turning point in American popular culture occurred in the mid-1950s whose effects persist to this day.

By then teenagers had money to spend on records and tickets, and the purveyors of entertainment were starting to target this audience. This meant that there was a mass market for themes that challenged established authority and rules of behavior.

In the decade before 1955, popular music was dominated by Broadway show tunes and soupy ballads such as "Secret Love" (1952). Black music meant Nat King Cole singing in French. Lyrics usually dealt with mature love and lifelong commitment.

Marshall Berman (on left) and Eugene Gaer

In 1954 a new genre emerged, characterized by rapid pace and heavy beat; it was a synthesis of black rhythm-and-blues music with country-and-western. At first denoted as "bebop," it soon became known as "rock and roll" for the way young people danced to it. The first rock-and-roll song on the popular charts, "Sh-boom," was rather tame, but a year later "Rock Around the Clock" by Bill Haley had all the key elements of early rock, especially a hard bass beat.

Rock and roll offered a sensual energy that was irresistible to teenagers across America, and later across the world. The subtext was assertion of the raw power of youth, and concomitant rejection of adult authority and mores.

At about the same time, several influential movies appeared that portrayed young men as strong, independent, and defiant of authority. Perhaps the best remembered today is *Rebel Without a Cause* starring James Dean, but *The Wild One* with Marlon Brando and *Blackboard Jungle* embodied similar themes. The latter film, whose theme song was "Rock Around the Clock," was the story of an idealistic teacher in a boys' trade school full of violent delinquents. Although the teacher, played by Glenn Ford, was clearly the hero, young males in the audience were more likely to identify themselves with the unruly students, especially given their common taste in music.

I was then a student at Steuben Junior High School at 52nd Street and North Avenue. All students were white at that time, and only a small percentage were Jewish. A lot of them were incipient juvenile delinquents, who called themselves "bops" after "bebop" music. Adults called them "punks" or "greasers" (for the grease in their hair). They wore pea-green tanker jackets, typically with a pack of cigarettes in one pocket and a switchblade knife in the other. The boys greased their hair, which often was combed into a "ducktail" at the back. I suspect that they were inspired in both their appearance and conduct by the rebellious teenagers portrayed in the popular culture.

I do not know if they ever really used the knives on anyone, but there were occasional fistfights around school and frequent talk of beating kids up. I was then shorter than most boys my age, overtly intellectual, and Jewish. For the three years I attended Steuben I was subjected to a good deal of harassment and bullying by the bops. Although I got slugged a few times, I was never really hurt. I avoided fighting back mainly for fear of getting a bad conduct record at the school.

My teachers were mediocre at best, and varied in their ability to control the classes. The most inept was a young English teacher who told his classes that he got through college by cheating. Our homeroom teacher referred to misbehaving pupils as "dirty *white* trash." A music teacher used the classroom radio to tune in Milwaukee Braves baseball broadcasts when there was no other pressing business, which was often.

I was then praying twice daily at Beth Jehudah and eating every Friday night with Rabbi Twerski and his family. At the same time, I was a typical American teenager going to public school, watching TV and movies, and listening to rock-and-roll music.

I had been listening to popular music for several years before the advent of rock. But by this time I had my own clock radio, which was always tuned to WRIT, 1340 AM, Milwaukee's premier rock-and-roll

station. Not only did I love the new sound, but the
lyrics about teenage crushes, school problems and
family difficulties often expressed my own thoughts.

So I was bombarded with a dissonance of conflicting
messages.

The message of Beth Jehudah was:

BE a good Jew.
BELIEVE that Man was created by G-d.
LISTEN to rabbinical lectures.
LEARN the Torah.
OBEY Jewish law.
COVER your head with a hat or yarmulke (skullcap).
DO NOT touch girls.

The message of Steuben Junior High School was:

BE a good student.
BELIEVE that Man was descended from apes.
LISTEN to announcements on the public address system.
LEARN the material in the textbooks.
OBEY school rules and your teachers.
HATS OFF in the school building.
DANCING with girls at supervised dances is OK.

The message of teen culture was:

BE a rebel.
LISTEN to rock-and-roll music.
LEARN to fight.
OBEY no rules or authorities
COVER your head with grease.
TOUCH girls as much as you can.

Of course, there was no way to reconcile these mutually contradictory viewpoints and imperatives.

One way out of the dissonance was to go to *yeshiva,* where messages inconsistent with Torah would be vigilantly screened out. My parents did not want me to attend *yeshiva,* but this was not the only reason I did not go there. I had already made considerable sacrifices for my Torah observance, but did not wish to trade my private room for a dormitory bed and give up my home life, television, movies, dating, and maybe even radio. My choice was to balance my personal needs and desires against the demands of an ideal; I chose a limited, rather than total, commitment. I have followed this pattern in many subsequent endeavors.

The problem I have termed "dissonance" between the teachings of Judaism and the messages of contemporary America has no general solution. Instead, there are several well-worn paths, and every Jew gets to choose among them.

Some orthodox Jews, especially *Chasidim,* take what I call the "Ghetto Path": immerse yourself in Torah and ignore everything else. Today significant numbers of young Jews are learning Yiddish as their first language, attend Chassidic day-schools and *yeshivas,* and reject college education. They read no English books, see no TV, hear no radio. Many consciously attempt to reconstruct the Jewish life of pre-20th-century Europe. How long can they avoid the challenges of the secular world just outside their doorsteps? If Borough Park in Brooklyn is any indication, quite a long while.

Another important group also believes in Torah, but chooses to engage the challenges of modern science. This group, termed "Modern Orthodox," is exempli-

fied by Yeshiva University of Manhattan, New York.
Maimonides was perhaps the first Modern Orthodox
Jew. The works of the late Rabbi Aryeh Kaplan have
inspired the Modern Orthodox to examine traditional
texts for evidence that supports, rather than denies,
modern discoveries. A key belief of Modern Orthodox, for example, is that Genesis provides a meta-
phorical (rather than literal) account of Creation; that
the "Days" mean "Eons." When the *Rebbe* sent his
sons to American secular universities, he set them on
a course unknown to his Chassidic forbears. As the
reader has no doubt surmised, I identify myself with
this viewpoint.

Many Jews of today, especially the young, have em-
braced modernism to the extent that they have rejected Judaism as well as al other forms of religious belief.
They are agnostic, and when they marry, the spouse
is usually a gentile agnostic. In the recent past, many
secularists replaced religious belief with some form of
Marxism, but today Marxism has also lost its appeal.
Within a generation or two, the descendants of these
people will have only the vaguest recollection of any
Jewish heritage at all.

Most American Jews desire neither assimilation nor
Orthodox observance. They affiliate with the Conservative and Reform branches of Judaism. These
groups offer a religion like more or less watered-down
chicken soup. They inspire no fervor or deep commitment, nor do they appeal to cold reason. If the Torah
was given by G-d, the Orthodox are right and there
is no reason to water down its commandments. If the
Torah was not given by G-d, there is no reason to be
Jewish at all and certainly no motivation to support a

rabbinate. Both Conservative and Reform are stuck on the horns of this dilemma, which I do not believe they can long survive. Some of the descendants of today's Conservative/Reform Jews will come back to Orthodoxy, and the rest will drift away into intermarriage and assimilation.

Washington High

Jack Nusan Porter, Sandy Aronin, and I all attended Milwaukee's Washington High School, located on Sherman Boulevard just south of West Center Street. The school, built in 1912, had previously educated a number of men who later became prominent, including U.S. Senator Herbert Kohl, Baseball Commissioner Bud Selig, actor Gene Wilder (then Jerome Silberman), and FCC Commissioner Newton Minow. But these future celebrities were all long gone when I entered in September, 1957.

The principal at that time was Arlie A. Schardt, who had been a colonel in the U.S. Army before turning to teaching and academic administration. Schardt was enamored of awards and pins, which he loved to bestow on worthy students. Hall monitors wore plain pins with the school colors (purple and gold); presidents of school clubs wore more impressive Student Leader pins. In 1958 Mr. Schardt created a Reader's Council, whose seven members got the best pins of all.

Most of the teachers were forgettable mediocrities, but my math teacher, Seymour Perchonok, was an exception. His love of mathematics was inspiring, and I enjoyed his classes so much that I majored in that subject in college. A short man (about 5 ft. 4 in.) with a slight Jewish accent, he loved quizzes and puzzles, and regaled his classes with them after finishing the required material for the class period. For example, he told us that his "Aunt Emma" liked boots, but not shoes. She also liked rubbers, but not galoshes. She liked "proceeding" but not "preceding." If you could guess three things that Aunt Emma did and did not like, you could join the Aunt Emma club. (Hint: she liked words with double letters!)

I also remember my Latin teacher, Mrs. Levin. One day she commented that words beginning with the letter "L" tended to mean bad things, such as "lewd, lascivious, licentious…" I added in an undertone "Levin, Latin…", which broke up the class. Although I was generally well behaved, I had a good deal of "chutzpah" (nerve) toward the faculty. Once, when I was using a long wooden pointer to show an algebra problem on the blackboard, I casually chalked up the point as though it were a pool cue. Anything for a laugh!

Washington High drew its student body from the northwest side of the City of Milwaukee, which at that time was virtually all white. (There was only one black student among the 2,400 enrolled during my first year at the school, and none thereafter. There were also a handful of people of Asian ancestry.) About a sixth of the students were Jewish (based on absence on Yom Kippur), with most of the rest of German heritage.

There were many after-school interest clubs, such as Science Club, Chess Club, Washington Players (drama club) and Future Teachers of America. There were also three debating clubs: Alphanea, Philomathea and

Lincoln. By custom, only Jews joined Lincoln, and only gentiles joined the other two. (One non-Jewish girl joined Lincoln by mistake one year, but it was no big deal.) The clubs did not debate each other, but had internal debates at every meeting. Whether "Red" China should be admitted to the United Nations was a popular topic.

One of the clubs under the aegis of the Reader's Council was devoted to political science. We decided to examine all points of view. We learned about socialism from the Socialist Mayor of Milwaukee, Frank P. Zeidler, and about communism by reading Karl Marx's *The Communist Manifesto.* The Milwaukee Journal covered our discussion on that topic, rather edgy for the Midwest in the '50s.

During my senior year I asked Mr. Schardt for permission to start a Math Club. He consented, but told me that the first year there would be no Student Leader pin for the president and no club picture in the yearbook. I recruited a young math teacher nicknamed "Euclid" Miller to be our advisor and was elected the first president. We were pictured in the yearbook, and I got a Student Leader pin! From this experience I learned to take what you could get, and maybe the rest would come later.

Most of the roughnecks that I went to Steuben Jr. High with did not go on to Washington High, which was then known as a high school for the college-bound. Most of them enrolled at our Boys Technical High School (now known as Bradley Tech). The "bops" who did go on to Washington High adapted to the culture of the school, and the fights and switchblades disappeared. I found the school rather pleasant and the academic work easy, so I rarely took a book home. I did all my homework in Study Hall, and devoted my evenings to TV, meetings, reading, and services at Beth Jehudah.

I skipped Senior English, since I knew that the course required a long term paper, which I considered an onerous imposition on my spare time. Older students warned me that I would not be prepared for college English, but I satisfied the English requirement at the University of Chicago by passing an entrance exam.

Although students of various white ethnicities attended classes together, once we left the school Jews hung out with Jews, and gentiles with gentiles. The B'nai B'rith in Milwaukee provided social clubs for Jewish teenagers: AZA (for boys) and B'nai B'rith Girls (BBG). The ostensible purpose of these groups was to prevent Jewish teens from dating, and perhaps later, marrying gentiles. For the most part, it worked.

Although some of my fellow students smoked and drank, there was no use of drugs. Some dates ended up with "heavy petting," but all the girls drew the line well short of intercourse. I can recall only one Washington High girl getting pregnant the entire three years I attended the school; today Washington High has a day-care center.

I could have joined AZA, but the program of sports and dances (with BBG) did not interest me at all. Instead I was attracted to a much smaller group of Jewish teens interested in Israel: Young Judea.

Young Judea

Young Judea (YJ) was a Zionist-oriented organization for teenagers sponsored jointly by the Zionist Organization of America (ZOA) and Hadassah. Meetings were held in the Hebrew School classrooms of Congregation Beth El Ner Tamid, then at 3725 N. Sherman Boulevard. Unlike the B'nai B'rith youth groups, there was no separation of boys and girls. The programs emphasized support for Israel, in the hope that members would become ardent Zionists in college and thereafter. A few even moved to Israel, although that was not the goal.

There were three chapters in Milwaukee, governed by a city council. There was a regional office in Chicago and a national office in New York. Regional, tri-regional and national conventions were held once per year.

Each chapter had a college-age advisor. Bert Kahn, who attended Beth Jehudah, was the advisor of the Mapilim chapter, and he recruited me to it in the spring of 1957. Some of the friendships that were formed during my years in YJ have lasted several decades.

The leader of Milwaukee YJ at that time was Eugene Gaer, a short, slim youth, whose parents (unlike mine) had been active in Zionist causes for years. His home, a large brick bungalow, was always filled with books and intellectual discussions. The youngest of three sons, Eugene learned fast and developed a fantastic memory, especially for history.

Another Young Judean was Jonathan Golan, who had spent part of his childhood living in Israel. His family name, Goldberg, was changed to Golan during that period, many years before the heights by that name were taken from Syria in 1967. Jonathan was also short, but rather stocky. He decided at a very young age to become a math professor, and never wavered from that course. Although brilliant, he was always a bit susceptible to conspiracy theories.

Seymour Pikofsky was one of only a few Young Judeans who did not live on the West Side or attend Washington High. His parents, substantially older than those of my other friends, had settled long ago in the area of 20th Street and Silver Spring Drive, before it was annexed to the City of Milwaukee. Seymour's father, even then well over 70, had known Golda Meir (then Mabowitz) during her early years in Milwaukee's Zionist community. Although Seymour was a little younger than me, he looked substantially older, since he was always heavy-set and needed to shave before any of his peers. Seymour attended Rufus King High School, and Young Judaea was his connection to Milwaukee's Jewish youth.

Lunchtime in the Washington High cafeteria was always cliquish, and we Young Judeans had our own table there. We attended the same meetings and parties, and developed close friendships, but there was no romantic involvement among the boys and girls in the group. We were more like siblings in a large family. However, I viewed the regional and tri-regional conventions as good opportunities to meet girls from other cities, and some of them were quite "hot." Although I and a girl from Detroit became "pen-pals" after the 1957 Tri-Regional, we were too far apart geographically for anything else.

Girls

I have always enjoyed the company of girls, and began dating even before high school. When I became orthodox I accepted many of the restrictions, such as keeping kosher and observing the Sabbath. But the total ban on touching girls, noted in the Dissonance section, was too much to ask of me, I have always been a loyal Jew, but never a perfect one.

Gerry and Cissy at their wedding

I developed an intense crush on one of Rabbi Twerski's granddaughters from Denver when her family spent several weeks in Milwaukee in the summer of 1956. She had wavy brown hair and a smile that seemed to light up an entire room.

Sandy Aronin got wind of my feelings for this girl. At that time Sandy was teaching me and some of the other younger guys a tractate of the Talmud known as *Arba Avos Nzikin* (Four Categories of Damages). He regaled anyone who would listen with this little song:

> *Glazer and little Miss Twerski*
> *Went together on a date,*
> *First they learned Arba Avos,*
> *Then began to osculate!*

If only it were true! After she returned home, I decided to write her a letter, but did not have her address. I managed to locate a boy in the synagogue who had it; he would give it to me if he could include a message to someone else staying at the same house. OK.

The message was, "Dear   : KMIT!" He told me that the message was in Yiddish and that the "M" stood for "Mir." My buddies and I puzzled over the message until we showed it to another guy, who solved it immediately: "Kish Mir in Toches" (Kiss My Ass).

In the spring in 1958, while visiting at the home of Bert Kahn and his family, I met a friend of his sister named Risa. She had long brown hair, bright green eyes and a really cute face. Risa was a few months older than me, which only made her more attractive. Although she was my date at my 16th birthday party, I soon learned that she liked guys who were older than her, not younger. She showed up at Beth Jehudah for *Simchas Torah* that year, and asked me to introduce her to my friend Yakov's older brother, then about 19. I introduced them, and within days she dumped me for the older guy.

While I was pursuing some cute girls without much luck, several other girls asked me out. None of this turned out good.

One was a sweet Christian girl, who asked me to a "Sady Hawkins Dance," where the girls asked the boys. I had to tell her that I dated only Jewish girls.

Another was a Jewish girl that I knew from school, but was not attracted to. She came up to me in a hallway at Washington High and said, "I have two tickets to the Winter Concert. Want to go?" Without thinking, I blurted out, "Sure, but who would I go with?" I took her.

Some of my friends were just as inept socially. One guy I'll call "Larry Smith" (not his real name) showed me a love letter he had written to a girl at school. It was signed, "Love, Larry Smith." I told Larry that if he had to sign his last name, he did not know the girl well enough to write her a love letter. He tore it up.

But while my efforts to find a girlfriend were not particularly successful, most of my best buddies were not dating at all.

Transition

Although Eugene was about my age, he graduated from Washington High a year before me, in June, 1959, and went off to Lawrence College. (He had skipped a semester in grade school, and took enough classes in summer school to gain another semester). At about the same time, Jonathan quit Young Judea. A number of younger kids were just joining then, but the group was no longer my crowd, so I quit too.

At that time I wanted to become a physicist, so I applied to the University of Chicago, where the first nuclear reactor had been built. In May of 1960 I was thrilled to receive a fat envelope from the Admissions Office offering me a scholarship. I was on my way.

Divergence

For a few years in the early 1950s the people portrayed in the preceding narrative were together in the Milwaukee Jewish community. We were influenced, and in turn our beliefs and actions have influenced others. By the end of the decade our paths had diverged, and many of us are now far apart, geographically and ideologically.

Rabbi Baumrind was fired by Congregation Beth Israel in 1957, when the synagogue switched to Conservative Judaism. He subsequently left Milwaukee, and died in Brooklyn, New York, in 1996.

Harry Garfinkel died in 1964. Thirty years later his formal pupils organized a reunion dinner at which his widow was guest of honor.

Rabbi Jacob Twerski, the Rebbe, died in August of 1973. He was then one of the few remaining links to the "shtetl" Jewry of Czarist Russia. But he also gave his sons the opportunity to attain success in purely American terms. As the founder of the American branch of the Twerski family and Congregation Beth Jehudah, his influence will be felt by American Jewry for generations to come. His kind will not pass this way again.

Rebbetzin Leah Twerski died in June, 1996, after a long illness. She was survived by 225 descendants, and will be remembered as the great Jewish Mother of the Beth Jehudah community. She was 95.

Motel Twerski and his family moved to Brooklyn in 1960, so that his growing sons could attend *yeshiva* near their home. He established a one-man accounting practice. On August 12, 1997, Motel suffered a dizzy spell while near the top of the stairway at his son Chaim's home in Chicago. He fell to the bottom, and his neck and spinal cord were broken. He was totally paralyzed, and lived in a rehabilitation center in New Jersey until his death in 1998. The accident occurred on *Tisha B'Av,* the saddest day of the Jewish year, just four months before the 40th anniversary of his near-fatal auto accident.

Rabbi Shea Twerski completed medical school with financial assistance from comedian Danny Thomas. While in medical school he composed a new melody for the verse from Psalms known in Hebrew as *"Hoshia Es Amecah,"* which was used without attribution on several Jewish record albums.

After receiving his M.D. degree, he moved to Pittsburgh and became a psychiatrist. he specialized in drug and alcoholism treatment, and founded the Gateway Rehabilitation Center there. He has written about 25 books, some on Jewish topics, others on "pop" psychology; many of the latter are illustrated with "Peanuts" cartoons. Shea often lectures on addiction and self-esteem. In his psychological works he maintains that a spiritual dimension is essential to a healthy personality. He now[5] lives in Lakewood, New Jersey.

Aaron Twerski went to Marquette University Law School in Milwaukee. After a stint in the US Department of Justice, he became a law professor. He now teaches at Brooklyn College Law School. He is a

Rabbi Michel Twerski and his wife Feige Twerski at Gerry's wedding

nationally recognized expert in the field of product liability, and was dean of the Hofstra University School of Law.

Michel Twerski became a rabbi in 1960, and returned to Milwaukee to succeed Shea as associate rabbi of Beth Jehudah. He soon became known as the composer of many melodies sung to Biblical or prayer quotations, including "Romimu," which is often heard at Jewish weddings. In 1971 he released an album of his most popular tunes, titled *A Voice on High in Romimu Stereo.* The Milwaukee Symphony Orchestra performed his music in a concert on July 6, 1997.

After the death of the Rebbe, Rabbi Michel became the sole spiritual leader of Beth Jehudah. He made special efforts to reach out to young Jewish couples that had little background in Torah. He not only spoke at forums, such as "Orthodox Perspective," but also invited interested people to his home for Sabbath meals and festivities. The bulk of his congregation today consists of people that he has recently influenced to become religious, just as I was so influenced by his family fifty years ago. He is known throughout American orthodox circles for his success at outreach activities, and audiotapes of his lectures are sold via mail-order from coast to coast. He founded the Yeshiva Elementary School and Milwaukee Kollel (adult education institute), both located in a former synagogue about a mile north of Beth Jehudah. His son, Rabbi Ben-Tzion (Tzini), is the third generation to lead the *shul.*

Yakov's total lack of self-discipline caused repeated anguish to his family, which is why I have not used his real name. When he was 18, he was expelled from *yeshiva* after he trapped a barefoot boy in the dormitory bathroom by scattering broken glass on the floor in front of the only door. Three years later he was expelled from the University of Wisconsin–Milwaukee after being arrested for gambling in the Math Department office. (This incident was reported in the local newspaper.) Subsequently, he married a non-Jewish girl. He became a programmer in California, then a city planner in Texas. I do not know where he is now.

Stanley (Meir) Schuster went to *yeshiva* after tenth grade, and continued Torah studies until he became a rabbi. In the mid-1960s he married and settled in Jerusalem, Israel. Since then he has devoted his life to bringing Torah education and observance into the lives of young Jews from nonobservant homes. At first he recruited prospective *yeshiva* students at the Western Wall. In 1971 he founded Heritage House, a youth hostel in Jerusalem. Thousands have passed through its doors since then, and I would venture that many Jews around the world are observant today because of their stay at Heritage House with Rabbi Schuster. I have heard that he now suffers from dementia.

Marshall Berman became a doctor, just as he had always hoped to do. He was inducted into the US Air Force as a doctor, and served briefly. After discharge he drifted from place to place and job to job without ever marrying or establishing a successful practice. He now lives in Los Angeles.

My Aunt Liz died in March, 2006.

Eugene Gaer went to Columbia University Law School after a few years of teaching history at

Roosevelt University in Chicago and West Liberty State College in West Virginia. He is now practicing law in Manhattan, and is also a hearing examiner for the New York Transit Authority. As of this writing, he is still single. We visit every time I come to New York, and we keep in touch by phone and e-mail between visits. Our friendship has lasted over half a century.

Jonathan Golan moved to Israel in 1967 and earned a Ph.D. in mathematics at Hebrew University. He married a daughter of a prominent Jerusalem family and fathered several children. Jonathan is now Professor of Mathematics at the University of Haifa, and has earned a reputation in the field of Ring Theory, a branch of higher algebra. I have had only sporadic contacts with him since he moved to Israel.

Seymour Pikofsky got married and became a lawyer in Milwaukee. More than any other Young Judean, he continued Zionist activity as an adult, and became a national officer of the Zionist Organization of America (ZOA). Unfortunately, he suffered dementia in his mid-sixties, and now lives in our Jewish nursing home.

Risa married an anesthesiologist, and sent her children to Hillel Academy, which my children attended at the same time. Last I heard, the couple lives in River Hills, Milwaukee's ritziest suburb.

The girl who asked me to the Winter Concert is still single.

I enrolled in the University of Chicago intending to become a physicist, but later changed my major to mathematics. After graduating in 1963, I went on to earn a master's degree in math at Northwestern University. While attending Northwestern I married

Cissy Cohen, a recent graduate of the Chicago Jewish Academy (now Ida Crown Academy). We settled in a Milwaukee duplex, just a few blocks from Beth Jehudah. We raised two boys and two girls. Both boys are now rabbis. One of our daughters is married to a rabbi, the other to a doctor. We have 28 grandchildren.

I taught college math for seven years at the University of Wisconsin at Waukesha. While teaching, I obtained a real estate license so that I could make some money during the summers, when teaching assignments were scarce. I did not hold a Ph.D., and was not accorded tenure. Accordingly, my employment at UWW ended in 1974, and I went to work for Mortgage Guaranty Insurance Company as a claims manager. After four years I saw that I was getting nowhere at MGIC, so I quit to sell real estate full-time. Although I also held some other jobs for a few years since then, I have sold over $22 million of real estate in my career, including the boyhood homes of Sandy, Yakov, the Twerskis, and Jack Nusan Porter, whose memoir appears in this publication.

When we settled into our present home in 1966, many Jews lived in our immediate area, as well as further south. The neighborhood was overwhelmingly white. Today, the neighborhood we live in is predominantly black, and the orthodox Jewish population of the West Side (now called the Sherman Park Area) has moved north of West Burleigh Street. The non-orthodox Jews have left Sherman Park, taking their two synagogues with them. Congregation Beth Jehudah moved to 52nd and Burleigh in May, 1999.

My father suffered a stroke on the eve of his 88th birthday in 2002, and has been living in the Milwaukee Jewish Home, a skilled-nursing facility, ever since. My mother died after a long illness on September 21, 2007.

Gerry Glazer Today

SANDY'S STORY

by
Sanford L. ("Sandy") Aronin

About 100 years ago the Aronin family came to
Wisconsin. Near the turn of the century, Rabbi Aryeh
Leib Aronin was sent by the Lubavicher Rebbe to
head the Jewish community of Sheboygan. Known as
"Little Jerusalem," Sheboygan, in 1900, boasted of
more than 250 Jewish families, who were recognized
all over the United States for their strict orthodoxy,
and three synagogues.

Subsequently, Rabbi Aronin's son, Shmuel (my
grandfather), sent for his cousin Leah Skolnick, and
they married on September 19, 1907. The Shmuel
Aronin family moved to Sturgeon Bay, where my father (of blessed memory) was born in 1912, then to
Fond du Lac and to Mayville. Shmuel was a peddler
and he moved where he could make a living to support my grandmother and their five sons. Mayville is
a small town, about a 45-minute drive northwest from
Milwaukee. At first, my father Jacob was an indepen-

dent peddler, who sold "merchandise" to Sam Aronin, "dealer in rags, scrap iron and metal." Eventually, my grandfather took him "into the business." Through his connections in Milwaukee, my father met and married Sadie Epstein on July 25, 1937. A year later, on July 29, I became a resident of the metropolis of Mayville with a population of about 2,700.

Although a few other Jewish families came and went, we were the only Jewish family living in Mayville for any length of time. Many of the inhabitants of Mayville were of German origin, so you can imagine the difficulties growing up as a Jew during and just after World War II. Moreover, either because I was bright (a Yiddishe kop) or because Miss Strampe would have had to teach me two years, both in second and third grades, I skipped second. So not only was I unique in my religion, I was a year younger (and smaller) than my classmates. Being a shy and quiet little boy, I got along well with most of them. In fact, some very close friendships developed. I remember pedaling my bike about three miles to visit my friend Franklin in Woodland, and I often played chess with Grant. However, some of my classmates who did not do well in school, and consequently had nothing in common with me, played their little pranks. I remember being beat up because I was "a dirty Jew." In fact, someone of little or no artistic talent had created a poem for me:

> *Sam Aronin, the Mayville Jew,*
> *Wiped his [expletive deleted] on the Mayville News.*
> *The paper tore, Sam's [deleted] got sore,*
> *And Sam [deleted] all over the bathroom floor.*

Another disadvantage of growing up in Mayville was a lack of formal Jewish education. It was tough to make a living in the 1920s and 1930s. Consequently, other than prayers and verses of the Bible, my grandfather was unable to educate his five sons formally. However, because he was strong in his beliefs and in his identity as a Jew, he did demonstrate much "Yiddishkeit" by example. And my grandmother instructed them with a Jewish mother's love. I remember when, on Shabbos, I used to visit my *Baba* and *Zeida* for lessons in *Chumash* (Pentateuch) and I would say (sometimes deliberately, I must confess) something to disturb him, *Baba* would try to calm the waters between us. In fact, because, as a result of studying with *Zeida*, I knew Yiddish so well, my grandparents had to speak in Russian if they didn't want me to understand their conversation.

I will relate for you an example of strong Jewish feelings being translated into improper action because

A rare picture of the Bobover Rebbe Halberstam (left), the Rebbetzin Twerski's brother, and his nephew, a young Motel Twerski, January 1961.

of a lack of formal Jewish education. *The Mayville News* was (and still is) a weekly newspaper. Mayvillians (I think that's what they are called) who wished a local daily paper had to subscribe to the *Fond du Lac Commonwealth Reporter*, which was delivered. To raise money, I had a paper route. During the week, I delivered the paper on my bicycle. When *Shabbos* came, I knew I couldn't ride my bike, so I pushed it.

Kosher meat came from Milwaukee. We ordered large quantities which we stored in the refrigerated locker at Lange's Meat Market. High Holy Services we attended at Congregation Beth Israel on Milwaukee's North Side near "Milwaukee Baba's" home. I sat next to my dad and davened as much as I could. Sometimes, I would visit my *Baba* at nearby Beth Medrash Hagodol, but I preferred the services at Beth Israel. There Cantor Moses Sorenson led a choir. I still remember his moving tune to the prayer *U'nesaneh Tokef,* and I sing it every year, hoping that a new *chazzan* would join me.

Pesach (Passover) was a real family holiday. We all ate at my grandparents' house. Matzos and other *Pesach* goodies again came from Milwaukee. However, milk was a local product. We drove to Clarks' Farm with our pails and watched as the milk flowed. Imagine *Cholov Yisroel* (Jewish milk) in Mayville.

When I reached the age of fourteen without celebrating my *bar mitzvah,* my parents decided it was time to move to Milwaukee so that my three siblings and I could have a formal Jewish education. To promote this goal we moved to 55ᵗʰ and Chambers, only three-and-a-half blocks from Congregation Beth Jehudah, otherwise known as Rabbi Twerski's *shul.*

Now when I had lived in Mayville, I sometimes visited Rabbi Twerski's *shul* on Milwaukee's North Side. In fact, my *Zeida* was a vice president of the congregation. There I had enjoyed the warmth of the rabbi and his sons. I remember that I had studied a prayer called *Ashrei*, and I could really say it fluently. So when Michel and Aaron, the twins, youngest of the Twerski boys, asked me to show my stuff, I recited *Ashrei.* Imagine my astonishment when they repeated the prayer at twice my speed.

But the *shul* had moved, and so had I. How would these moves change my religious life?

I remember walking proudly to *shul* on *Shabbos,* carrying my rayon *talis* (scarf). I did not realize at the time what this *talis* would symbolize to me in the future. Under the influence of the Twerskis I learned that we don't carry outdoors on *Shabbos.* Also, because the *talis* was too small to cover a person properly, I abandoned this form of dress, substituting an *arba konfos* (four-cornered garment) worn under my shirt.

Came the fall, and I enrolled as a sophomore in (Rah! Rah!) Washington High School. After my high-school classes, I attended Beth Jehudah Hebrew School. Rabbi (now also Doctor) Abraham Joshua Twerski (affectionately known as Shea) was to be my teacher. Although my Hebrew was limited to a few words from the *Chumash,* he immediately placed me in a *Talmud* class with boys my own age. These young men had much more experience in Hebrew studies than I, but I tried to fit in. With Shea's word lists to buoy me up, I began to swim in the *Yam HaTalmud,* the sea of the Talmud.

My classmates, Bert and Shamshy, were very supportive, and I felt very comfortable in my new environment.

This next episode I have successfully blocked out of my memory, but since I have heard it many times, it must be true. One day, I brought a squirt-gun to the *shul* and dampened the spirits of my *Talmud* class, including the teacher, Rabbi Twerski. I don't remember the consequences of my actions, but they could not have been fatal.

I remember another example of the "shtick" I performed in Milwaukee in my youth. Shea's older brother, Mordechai Dov Ber (Motel) was an accountant. In Milwaukee, before *Pesach,* he opened a temporary enterprise known as Motel Twerski's Passover Store. For several weeks, a Jew could obtain for the holiday all the necessities (and many luxuries) for a week of feasting — and in one place. The Store even took orders by phone. Aaron and Sonya Richt, the *shul's* sexton and his wife, *aleihem hashalom,* assisted on the phone.

Rabbi Jacob Twerski looking at Sandy Aronin's wedding pictures.

One evening, Mrs. Richt received a lengthy order: lotsa matzah, sour salt, Hungarian deluxe, etc., etc., etc. She was delighted to take a such a large and expensive order — until she recognized my voice. "Sender [my Yiddish name], the *meshuganer!"* she exclaimed. This incident I do remember clearly.

Even during the secular part of the day, during school hours, I was able to "grow up Jewish in Milwaukee." Many times during the school year I brought my lunch to Bert's grandmother's apartment. There Bert's cousin Stuart joined us. Consequently, we had a *mezumen,* a quorum of three, to *bentch* (to say grace after meals) as a group. This was probably illegal. Those were the days when schools had rules. Students of Washington High could eat in only two places, at home or in the school cafeteria. And technically, we were at neither of these two places. but with the experience we had received from studying *Talmud,* we were able to rationalize that we were eating in our quasi-home.

Sometimes I would pedal my bike to Mayville Baba's home (she had become another "Milwaukee Baba") for lunch. There she served delicious chicken and chicken soup, with the noodles cooked in the soup. This gave them the taste of chicken and made them very soft. For dessert, I ate her dark chocolate cake. What a treat!

One day, I decided to take up a cause. The rayon *talis* that I had abandoned early in my Jewish "career" was really improper to wear. People who sold them to other Jews or who kept them on hand in *shul* for others to borrow and to make a *brochoh* (blessing) thereon were aiding those uneducated Jews in pronouncing a *brochoh l'vatalah*, an improper blessing. These *talesim* were really "enemies of Judaism." Therefore, I developed a symbol, a rayon *talis* pierced by a dagger, and posted these symbols, captioned "Enemy of Judaism," throughout the *shul*. However, I don't think that their sale and use were affected.

As the name "Aronin" — derived from Aaron, the High Priest — may suggest, we are *Kohanim,* descendants of Aaron. When Shea's son Yitschok was born, Shea had to prepare for a *Pidyon HaBen,* redemption of the first-born, where he would "purchase" his firstborn son from a *Kohain* for five silver dollars, as commanded in the Torah. Because some people feel that down through the ages the identity of a *Kohain* may have been lost or made invalid through an improper marriage, Shea decided to honor many members of his congregation by choosing each as *Kohain.* Surely at least one will be an authentic *Kohain!* I was one of the privileged few. And my *Zeida* was also chosen, except he was given a five-dollar gold piece.[6] Some of my friends commented that this was really unnecessary: if my *Zeida* were not a *Kohain,* neither was I. But I did not turn down the opportunity to participate in my Rebbe's *simcha.*

Other than Bert, Stuart and Shamshy, I had other Jewish friends at Washington High School. One friend showed me his birth certificate. It was written in three languages: English, Hebrew and Arabic. He was a Sabra, born in Israel. He was very knowledgeable in things Hebrew: his father was an important person in Milwaukee's Board of Jewish Education. Yet I was shocked: he wasn't very observant. While many of my friends and I missed school for Jewish holidays, such as *Pesach* and *Succos*, he attended. And he teased me for taking off.

In the 1955 Washington High School Scroll, our yearbook, he penned:

> *To the greatest poet of them all, it's really been great knowing you, with our brilliant discussions of big and little infinity and such. You are a swell guy, and your humor helps. I really admire your convictions, but tolerance is also a good characteristic to have…*

I learned a lesson that would stay with me: no matter how our more liberal co-religionists act towards us: whether they mock our adherence to the G-d given Torah of our ancestors, or they call us old-fashioned fanatics, we must be tolerant.

Other friends I met at Washington High were Ben, who shared my love of Latin (Pax vobiscum!); Joe, a fellow sousaphone player in the band; and Jerry, whom I defeated to become the Chess Champion of Sherman Playground. And, of course, I mustn't forget Gerry Glazer, with whom I also played chess and spent many hours in shul.

Milwaukee presented many opportunities to turn secular matters into holiness. One afternoon, Michel, Aaron and I decided to attend a Milwaukee Braves game at County Stadium. We were about to witness the great stars, Billy Bruton, Waren Spahn and Eddie Matthews, write new pages in baseball history. Then it began to rain. Out came our *Tanachs* (biblical books of the Prophets and Writings), and we studied the Book of Joshua.

Motel was a *mashgiach (kashrus* supervisor) at a cheese factory. His task was to drive to the factory, drop the kosher *rennet* into the hot milk, and wait until the mixture became "curds and whey." One day he asked me to accompany him (what Wisconsin boy wouldn't want to help produce cheese?). While we were waiting, Motel pulled out his *Noda B'Yehudah* (a book of religious *responsa* written by Rabbi Y-chezk'el Landau [1713-93]), and we delved into complex theories of interpreting testimony of witnesses. Many times since have I used these thoughts in my *Talmud* studies. Thanks, Motel!

Now here was a young boy who came to Milwaukee with very little Jewish or Hebrew knowledge and a few years later was studying rabbinic *responsa.* How and why?

First, I must have realized my lack of understanding of my heritage. Of all my new friends, only I had never celebrated a *bar mitzvah.* Also, I now knew that my parents had made the sacrifice of moving an hour's drive from my father's business, and I didn't want this to be in vain. But most of all, I had G-d's help. It

From left, three sons of the Rebbe Twerski---Aaron, Shea, and Michel

doesn't take a village to raise a Jew, only a loving and dedicated family, the Twerskis. Who was Rabbi Jacob Twerski, the head of a new dynasty of rabbis and dedicated Jews?

Rabbi Twerski was kind and understanding, and he possessed a great sense of humor. A few personal examples follow.

As the "chief rabbi" of Milwaukee, Rabbi Twerski was known to many, many Jews in Milwaukee and the world. Before Rosh Hashanah, his card list was very long, and he hired some of the neighborhood kids to address his Rosh Hashanah cards. I was included among the chosen few. As the number of cards sent was enormous, a few returned because they were addressed wrong or the recipient had moved. Rabbi Twerski told me that the post office had known that I was responsible for addressing these returned cards. Then he showed me the message stamped on them: "Return to Sender [my Yiddish name]."

As I entered my twenties, still a bachelor, Rabbi Twerski offered to use numerology to determine my future wife's name. Each Hebrew letter has a numeric equivalent. So, Rabbi Twerski instructed me to add the letters in my name, those in my father's name and my mother's name. Then he asked me to add some other numbers and give him the total. I did so. He paused and smiled. "Your wife's name," he announced, "will be 'Mrs. Aronin'!" And it was.

For three years, I was receiving the best of two worlds. My time at Washington High School was very productive: math and science were fun, and I enjoyed writing essays in English classes. Two years of bookkeeping would influence my career plans.

In the meantime, at Beth Jehudah Hebrew School, the teachings of Shea and the influence of his brothers made my study of Torah very enjoyable and desirable. I always looked forward to Shea's next lesson. But the good G-d had other plans for me.

One day my Rebbe (Shea) announced that he felt that he could better serve the Jewish community through the field of medicine. Consequently, he enrolled in the medical school of Marquette University. This decision meant that he would no longer be able to teach and inspire Talmud at Beth Jehudah Hebrew School. I was devastated. Where could my new thirst for Torah be quenched?

My first reaction was to draw a sign picturing my "enemy of Judaism" and post it on Shea's front door. In my young eyes, he had become a true enemy of *my* Judaism. But this did not solve my problem.

I consulted with my friends Michel and Aaron to discover other ways to advance my Hebrew and Talmud studies. The most practical and viable alternative was the Hebrew Theological College on Chicago's West Side. The Twerski twins spent much of their summer that year supervising my studies. If I were to pass the Yeshiva's entrance exam and get into a good class, I would really have to learn well. We decided on a small tractate of the Talmud, *Makos.* My 1955 summer vacation was now determined.

Meanwhile, I convinced my dear parents that my decision was wise. To really spend time at Yeshiva productively, I would have to devote much time. This meant postponing my college classes at least a semester. However, some of the time would be made up by the college elective credits the Hebrew classes would yield. And after all, we moved to Milwaukee to give us a Jewish education.

While I studied in the Yeshiva, I learned customs that differed with my newly acquired way of life in Milwaukee. For example, I learned from the Twerskis that on the day after *Succos, Shmini Atzeres,* one does not eat in a *succah.* In *yeshiva* I was taught that because there is a possibility that the day we celebrate *Shmini Atzeres* may actually be the last day of *Succos,* we sit in the *succah* but we don't make the *brocho* on the *succah.*

During one of my visits home from the *Yeshiva* for *Succos,* I was invited to the Twerskis for lunch on *Shmini Atzeres.* Thanks to Motel giving us his old *succah* when he acquired a new one, the Aronins had a *succah* at home; but I didn't want to turn down an opportunity to eat at a Rebbe's *tish* (table). Immediately after the morning services, I made my way to the *succah* in the *shul.* There I sat and waited — and waited — and waited. Nobody joined me.

Finally one of the Twins came out to summon me into the house. "But," I protested, "we should eat in the *succah!*"

The answer startled me: "You are exempt from the *succah.* If you stay here you won't be fed and you'll be in pain. A person in pain because he sits in the *succah* is exempt from *succah!*"

I also remember another Milwaukee Twerski custom. On *Simchas Torah,* the day for rejoicing with the Torah, after *Maariv,* the evening prayer, the *mechitza* (partition between the genders in *shul)* would be removed. People of all backgrounds would gather near the front to watch Rabbi Twerski and his sons (and

91

the few *Yeshiva* boys home for *Succos)* dance with the
Torah, singing lively and traditional songs. For the
Jews of Milwaukee at that time, giving honor to the
Torah after spending a major portion of life studying
it was a "spectator sport." A relic from the olden days
of Europe, these actions were to be witnessed as one
views a display in a museum: interesting, but not rel-
evant to daily life. Although I haven't spent *Simchas
Torah* in Milwaukee for thirty years, I can safely state
that times and attitudes have changed. Now Milwaukee has a *yeshiva* of its own, the Wisconsin Institute
for Torah Studies (WITS), a *kollel* for advanced Torah studies, and Yeshiva Elementary School (YES).
The teachers and students of these Torah institutions,
along with their families and friends, comprise a large
core of Jews who love and appreciate Torah learning.
They truly find joy in the Torah.

I must confess that when I returned to Milwaukee
after my year at HTC on the West Side, two productive years at Yeshivas Ner Israel in Baltimore, Mary-
land, and many more good years of studying at HTC,
which had moved to a new campus in Skokie, Illinois,
these schools had not yet been formed in Milwaukee.
As I had been graduated from Chicago's Roosevelt
University with a degree in accounting, my parents
and I decided that it was time for me to begin earn-
ing a living. Of course, my first choice for job-hunting
was my hometown, Milwaukee.

On my many visits home from *yeshiva,* I met Rabbi
Michel Twerski's children's baby-sitter, Ayala. Ayala
was a tall young lady, olive-skinned with a brilliant
smile and a cute pointy nose. An Israeli, she had a cute
accent, too. And she lived a block away.

Quite often I drove her to school at Washington High (Rah! Rah!). Being a gentleman, I helped her don her coat on cold days. It was quite a stretch, for she was several inches taller than me. Once I asked her to a movie, the Beatles' *Yellow Submarine.* One day she decided that we should "be friends." The article announcing her engagement was illustrated with a picture of her that I had taken.

I had scheduled my job interviews so as not to interfere with my "taxi services." One such interview resulted from a City Service Exam for the level of Acct I – Audit I. I placed second on the listing of those who had taken the exam, with a score of 89.82. But I was rejected because I had no experience. Then I scheduled an interview with the business of a prominent member of the *shul.* Word got back to me that one of the reasons I didn't get this position was because I insisted on wearing a skullcap at the interview. Anti-Semite!

After these and other disappointments, I decided to try Chicago to continue my search. I wrote my alma mater, Roosevelt, and received a list of accounting firms that had interviewed on campus. I chose Checkers, Simon & Rosner, and they accepted me. I moved to Chicago and shared a two-room apartment with other former Yeshiva students in Chicago's Albany Park area.

Of course, I visited Milwaukee very often. And Milwaukee was yet to play another great part in my Jewish life. One day I visited Michel, who lived with his family across 55th Street from my parents' home. Rebbetzin Twerski (née Feige Stein) told me that she had met a beautiful girl at her father's *shul* in Bensonhurst, Brooklyn, and that I should fly to New York to meet her.

Meanwhile, in Seattle, Washington, Margaret Frand decided to attend Stern College for Women in New York City. As she was the last of the Frand kids to leave, her younger brother, Allan,[7] had left for Ner Israel in Baltimore after his *bar mitzvah,* her parents moved to the big city, settling in Bensonhurst, which allowed trees to grow, a few houses away from Rabbi Israel Stein. Being a domestic young lady, she often was in the kitchen of Rabbi Stein's *shul,* helping out. And this is where Feige Twerski met her. "Are you engaged?" was the first question she asked Margaret. On receiving a negative reply, she announced: "I have a nice boy for you!"

For a while, Margaret was learning about this "nice boy" when Feige came to New York, and I was hearing about Margaret when I would visit Milwaukee. Finally, I decided to pay New York a visit with a list, which included Margaret's name and address. Our first meeting made a great impressin on me. I was very impressed with her parents. Hungarian-born but absorbing the culture of Frankfurt, Germany, they exuded class. Mr. Frand, *olov hashalom,* an accountant for Barton's Chocolate, was a very kind gentleman with a sense of humor. I immediately liked him. Margaret's mother gave me the impression of a very strong woman with classical tastes. And Margaret, a beautiful young lady with a beguiling smile, was a true product of German class and Hungarian warmth.

Our first date was the first night of *Slichos.* I "popped the question" on the BMT (Brooklyn subway) during Thanksgiving weekend. (I couldn't afford the plane tickets and the phone bills!)

Now we are the proud parents of four offspring. Shmuel is married to Nechama, and they are the parents of Daniel Yaakov (named after my father, Yaakov) and are both into computers. Shmuel spends his free evenings in a *kollel,* studying Torah.

Shelley inspires preschoolers at a Jewish community center. She is married to Berish, who is studying for ordination at the Hebrew Theological College. They are the parents of my beautiful granddaughter Chani.

Shanni is the artist of the family. She is a senior at Columbia College in Chicago, majoring in graphic design. She recently designed the cover of a pamphlet on Jewish law that I've written.

Dovid is a senior at Fasman Yeshiva High School of the Hebrew Theological College.

As I grew up Jewish in Milwaukee and Margaret grew up Jewish in Seattle, our children are growing up Jewish in Chicago!

Sandy Aronin today, carrying the Torah

Congregation Beth Jehudah Sisterhood
2700 NORTH 54TH STREET

Rabbi Jacob Twerski
1898 - 1973
(5658) - (5733)

the "Rebbe"—Rabbi Jacob Twerski (1898-1973)

NOTES

1.) See pages 8-11 of the Porter memoir for more about Beth Israel and the Academy.

2.) See pages 83-94 of the Aronin memoir for more about the Twerskis.

3.) See page 84 of the Aronin memoir for confirmation of this.

4.) "Jack-ankle" was a euphemism for "jackass" derived from the song parody "On top of Old Smoky / All covered with glass / I stepped on a pebble / And fell on my ankle." (By the way, in 1956, "queer" meant nothing more than "strange")

5.) March, 2010.

6.) See the book *Generation to Generation* by Abraham J. Twerski, pages 53-54.

7.) The world-famous Rabbi Yissacher Frand, author and lecturer; you can receive him on the Internet.

GLOSSARY OF JEWISH/YIDDISH TERMINOLOGY

aleihem hashalom — "May he or she rest in peace", said after someone has died

Amidah — a standing prayer

arba konfos — four-cornered garment worn under a shirt on *Shabbos.*

Ashrei — a Jewish prayer

Baba — Yiddish for grandma

bar mitzvah — you know what that is

bentch — say grace after meals.

B'nai B'rith — a Jewish men's organization

bris mila — circumcision.

brochoh — blessing.

brochoh l'vatalah — improper blessing.

bronfm — whiskey.

Chasidim — frum followers of a rebbe

chazzan — cantor.

Cholov Yisroel — Jewish milk, kosher milk.

Chumash — Pentateuch, or the first five books of the Torah.

chutzpah — nerve.

davening — praying.

freilich — happy.

frum — religious, in an Orthodox way.

greeneh — "greenhorns," slang for European refugees.

Habonim — "The Builders" in Hebrew, a Labor Zionist youth movement

Hoshia Es Amecah — a prayer, "Save Your People" Psalms 28:9

Ichud Habonim — see Habonim

kashrus — Yiddish for kosher, according to Jewish food laws

kibbutz — a collective farm/institution in Israel

Kohain — descendant of Aaron. (Plural: *Kohanim)*

kollel — adult education institute.

Maariv — the evening prayer.

Makos — punishments

Mar — Mr. in Hebrew

mashgiach — *kashrus* supervisor.

mechitza — the partition between the genders in *shul.*

menschleich — gentlemanly-like

meshuganer — crazy

mezumen — a quorum of three.

minyan — ten men.

Noda B'Yehudah — book of religious *responsa* written by Rabbi Y-chezk'el Landau (1713-93)

olov hashalom — "to go up in peace", said after a deceased person's name

Onegei Shabbat — Sabbath joy

Pesach — Passover.

Pidyon HaBen — redemption of the first-born in the family.

Rebbe — a special rabbi with many Chassidim, followers

rebbetzin — rabbi's wife.

rennet — a product that curdles milk

responsa — a book of answers to religious questions

Romimu — a Jewish prayer and song; "Exalt!" Psalms 99:5

"Roni V'simchi" haftarah — the prophet section sung by the bar mitzvah boy or today, also the bat mitzvah girl—it was Jackie Porter's haftarah

Rosh Ken — Literally *"head of the nest" in Hebrew; president of the local Habonim group*

Sabra — an Israeli by birth.

Shabbos — the Sabbath

shaliach — messenger, emissary

shamus — administrator.

Shmini Atzeres — the day after *Succos.*

Shoah — the Holocaust

shteiblach — "religious houses" in Yiddish.

shtreimel — a cylindrical fur hat Chassidic rabbis wear on the Sabbath and holidays.

shul — a synagogue or Jewish place of worship.

Shulchan Aruch — *a book of Jewish laws*

simcha — a festive occasion, like a wedding

Simchas Torah — the day for rejoicing with the Torah.

Slichos — prayers said before the High Holy Days

succah — *a hut or shed*

sukkah (plural, Sukkos or Sukkot) — a special hut or shed covered with vegetation, used to celebrate the holiday of Succos (Tabernacles), in which the Children of Israel lived while in the desert, per Numbers 29:12.

Sukkos — Tabernacles, huts, sheds, shelter—also the name of the Jewish holiday in Yiddish; Sukkot in Hebrew.

talis (Plural: **talesim**)---Fringed prayer shawl for men, worn in accordance with Numbers 15: 37-41

Talmud — the oral law compiled into many volumes

Tanach — biblical books of the Prophets and Writings.

t'fillin — leather-bound boxes of parchment.

tish — table.

Tisha B'Av — 9th day of the Hebrew month Av (late summer), on which both Temples in Jerusalem were destroyed, now a day of mourning and fasting for the Jews

U'nesaneh Tokef — important High Holy Day prayer

Yam HaTalmud — "the sea of the Talmud."

yarmulke — skullcap.

yeshiva — rabbinical school.

Yizkor — the time of remembrance of the dead, especially *Shoah* dead.

Yom Kippur — Day of Atonement

Zeida — Yiddish for grandpa

SELECTED BIBLIOGRAPHY

Austin. H. Russell. *The Milwaukee Story: The Making of an American City.* Milwaukee, WI: The Milwaukee Journal Company, 1946. An interesting history of the city published in the year we came to America but with little mention of Jews.

Barth, Jack. *Roadside Hollywood.* Chicago, IL: Contemporary Books, 1991. A state-by-state exhibit of movies made, film locations, celebrity hangouts, and tourist attractions. The Wisconsin and Milwaukee section is on pp. 91-95.

Berman, Hyman, and Linda Mack Schloff. *Jews in Minnesota.* St. Paul, MN: Minnesota Historical Society Press, 2002. Since my sister Bella Porter-Smith and my mother Faye Porter-Arenzon moved from Milwaukee to Minneapolis, I include this other Midwestern state as a kind of comparison. Very useful.

Bowie, Beverley M. and Volkmar Wentzel. "Wisconsin: Land of the Good Life," *The National Geographic Magazine,* vol. CXI, no. 2, pp. 141-187. A neat and quite comprehensive view of the entire state, and especially "Mahn-a-waukee Seepe," Indian for "gathering place by the river," plus its German and ethnic background.

Breslau, David (editor). *Adventure in Pioneering: The Story of 25 Years of Habonim Camping.* New York: The Chay Commission of the Labor Zionist Movement, 1957. The 25th anniversary, 1932-1957, of the youth movement Habonim-Dror, which I attended from 1955 to 1965. See pp. 93-97 on Midwest Camp

103

Habonim, on Kaiser Lake, in Three Rivers, Michigan, in the southern part of the state, near Kalamazoo, the camp I attended as a youngster.

Buege, Bob. *The Milwaukee Braves: A Baseball Eulogy,* forward by Eddie Mathews. Milwaukee, WI: Douglas American Sports Publications, 1988, paperback. A marvelous play-by-play, year-by-year account of the craziness that overtook Milwaukee from 1952-1965, but especially 1952-1959, my years as a Braves fan. See also Jeffrey Saint and John Stuart, *Twilight Teams: 1952 Boston Braves,* Gaithersburg, MD: Sark Publishing, 2000, and the Boston Braves Historical Association. The Braves came from Boston to Milwaukee in 1953.

Corenthal, Michael G. *Mr. Michael's Czarina Kid and Other Weird Tales.* Milwaukee, WI: MGC Publications, 1995. A glossy paperback introduction to the weird yet genius world of Mike Corenthal. Billed as "Mr. Mike's First Milwaukee Omnibus," I don't recognize his version of the West Side, but there it is.

Esselin, Alter. *Poems by Alter Esselin.* Translated from the Yiddish by Joseph Esselin. Chicago, IL: Interface, 1968. Privately published by Joseph Esselin, 1211 North La Salle St., Chicago, IL 60610.

Fleckner, John A., and Stanley Mallach (editors). *Guide to Historical Resources in Milwaukee Area Archives.* Milwaukee, WI: Milwaukee County Historical Society, 1976. An excellent source, though a bit dated, for research.

Fly, Colin. "Frank Zeidler, 93, former mayor of Milwaukee," *Boston Sunday Globe,* July 9, 2006, p. B8. An obituary written by an Associated Press reporter on the former mayor, who was the last Socialist to run a major American city.

Geenen, Paul H. *Images of America: Milwaukee's Bronzeville 1900-1950.* Charleston, SC, and other cities: Arcadia Publishing, 2006. This is a glossy photo book in the *Images of America* series. We called it the "inner city." Bronzeville was the African-American name for the same place. It's interesting that they stop in 1950 when the Jews and other whites left the inner city and Blacks moved in. I wish there had been more on the Jewish-to-Black transition, but it does include one telling photo (p. 170) of Jacob Goldberg's Drugstore in 1920 at Tenth and Walnut, which had a second-floor apartment where Vel Phillips lived. She was the first African-American woman to serve on Milwaukee's Common Council, the first African-American judge, and the first African-American Secretary of State in Wisconsin, and arguably the last. She was active in the 1950s and 1960s. I learned a lot from this book.

Gurda, John. *One People, Many Paths: A History of Jewish Milwaukee.* Milwaukee, WI: Jewish Museum of Milwaukee, 2009. The major history of the Milwaukee Jewish community frm 1844-2009, building on the shoulders of the famous Rabbi Louis Swichkow and Lloyd Gartner book. Sadly, I, my family, Andy Muchin, and many others never made it into the book, which is a bit weak in the cultural, artistic and academic/intellectual life of the community but otherwise quite comprehensive. He doesn't miss much. Also see his *The Making of Milwaukee* and the companion public television series based on it.

Hachten, Harva, and Terese Allen. *The Flavor of Wisconsin: An Informal History of Food and Eating in the Badger State.* Revised and expanded edition. Madison, WI: Wisconsin Historical Society Press, 2009. First published in 1981, this magnificent book contains a wonderful history and sociology of foods from fish boils to oleomargarine fights to cheese battles to recipes for kartoffel and matzo balls. As one person put it, every state should have such a book.

Hintz, Martin. *Images of America: Jewish Milwaukee.* Charleston, SC, and other cities: Arcadia Publishing, 2005. A glossy paperback of photos. Page 81 has a picture of my father, second row, second from left, of the Fruit Peddlers Union, but does not mention him and erroneously states that it was taken before World War II. In fact, the picture was *after* the war, since we did not come to America until 1946. The picture actually dates from about 1950. Most of these "fruit peddlers" later became scrap-metal dealers, which was much more lucrative.

Leuchter, Sara, and Jean Loeb Lettofsky (editors). *Guide to Wisconsin Survivors of the Holocaust: A Documentation Project of the Wisconsin Jewish Archives.* Madison, WI: The State Historical Society of Wisconsin, 1983. Based on the Wisconsin Jewish Archives, here I found people I knew: Walter

Peltz (pp. 51-52), Cyla Stundel (pp. 59-60), Israel Wolnerman (pp. 64-65), and Sylvia Blasberg (pp. 21-23).

Olivo, Frank J. *Musical Memories 1930-1970,* no place or city of publication, 1975. An entertaining list of "hits" from 1930 to 1970. Much research went into this booklet.

Perlson, Edwarde F. "Walnut Street in the 1920s: Grand in Many Ways," *Wisconsin Jewish Chronicle,* December 5, 1980, section II, pp. 12-15. A rare description by a veteran Jewish journalist from Milwaukee of the old north side, the Walnut Street entry point for the Jewish community. Sadly, hardly anything remains Jewishly there today.

Porter, Jack Nusan. *If Only They Could Bottle It: Memoirs of a Radical Son.* In progress, 2010. Jack Porter's memoirs.

Ruby, Marilyn. "Calendar Highlights Diversity of Sherman Park, *Wisconsin Jewish Chronicle,* December 24, 1993, page 2. A story about the "diversity calendar" featuring Rabbi Michel Twerski, my mother Faye Porter-Arenzon, and many others, clergy to students to butchers, nearly all make up the West Side today.

Shapiro, David S. *Studies in Jewish Thought.* New York: Yeshiva University Press, 1975. A collection of theological essays by the eminent Milwaukee rabbi.

Stevens, Michael E., and Ellen D. Goldlust-Gingrich (editors). *Voices of Wisconsin Past:*

Remembering the Holocaust. Madison, WI: State Historical Society of Wisconsin, 1997. Some of the memoirs and people I know are Manfred Swarsensky and Walter Peltz (pp. 94-112).

Swichkow, Louis J. and Lloyd P. Gartner. *The History of the Jews of Milwaukee.* Philadelphia, PA: Jewish Publication Society, 1963. The standard textbook until the John Gurda book was written — dull, sober, but thorough.

Traxler, Ruth. *The Golden Land: 150 Years of Jewish Life in Milwaukee.* Milwaukee, WI: The Milwaukee Jewish Federation, Sesquicentennial Celebration, 1994. A nice overview with lovely photos of 150 years of Jews in Milwaukee. Mention of my family is on page 13 and of me on page 60. The old West Side days are mentioned on pp. 52-54 and 86-99.

Wilder, Gene. *Kiss Me Like a Stranger: My Search for Love and Art*. New York: St. Martin's Press, 2005. Contains some rare photos and memorabilia of Mr. Wilder's days on the old west side of Milwaukee, a very lovely look into the life of a very lovely and talented man. See pages 7-31 especially on Milwaukee.

Widen, Larry, and Judi Anderson. *Silver Screens: A Pictorial History of Milwaukee's Movie Theaters.* Madison, WI: Wisconsin Historical Society Press, 2007. A glossy paperback of all the wonderful movie theaters in Milwaukee, nearly all of them gone. Note the Sherman and Uptown Theater of the old West Side; the Uptown is mentioned in Gene Wilder's memoir on page 9.

Wisconsin Jewish Publications Foundation and Wisconsin Jewish Chronicle. *The Jewish Community Handbook*, 5737. Milwaukee, WI: Wisconsin Jewish Chronicle, 1976. A number of such handbooks came out in the 1970s and continue to be published yearly, and are useful guides to the community.

ABOUT THE AUTHORS

Jack Nusan Porter was born in Rovno, Ukraine on December 2, 1944, spent time in the Bindermichel DP Camp near Linz, Austria from June 1945 to July 1946, and arrived in Milwaukee in the fall of 1946. Attended Milwaukee Public Schools, graduated Washington High School in June 1962, went to Israel for a year, and then attended University of Wisconsin-Milwaukee from 1963-1967, majoring in sociology. Did graduate work in sociology at Northwestern University from 1967-1971, where he gained his Ph.D.

He has been a college professor, writer, editor, Holocaust scholar, rabbi, and real estate broker in a varied career. He now lives in Newtonville, Mass near his two children, Gabe and Danielle.

His many books include *The Sociology of American Jews, Women in Chains: On the Agunah*, and *Jewish Radicalism*. His future book projects include *Milwaukee, and Hollywood, If Only You Could Bottle It* (a memoir), and *Solomon and Sheba: Essays on Blacks and Jews*. For more on his life, see his entry in Wikipedia and his website at <www.drjackporter.com>; he can be contacted at jacknusan@earthlink.net

Gerry Glazer was born in Milwaukee on September 26, 1942, attended Milwaukee Public Schools, graduated Washington High School in June 1960, received his BS from the University of Chicago in 1963, his MS from Northwestern University in 1965 (both in math), and additional graduate study at UW-M in 1966-1967.

He was an instructor of mathematics at UW-Waukesha (1967-1974), claims manager at MGIC (1974-1978), and real estate broker since 1971. He has sold over $22 million worth of real estate, including the boyhood homes of Jackie Porter and Sandy Aronin.

Married to the former Cissy Cohen since 1965, he has four children and 28 grandchildren. He can be reached at gsglazer@sbcglobal.net

Sandy Aronin was born in Mayville, WI in 1938 and moved to Milwaukee, graduating from Washington High School in June 1955. He attended Chicago Yeshiva and Roosevelt University with a degree in accounting. Worked as an accountant for the firm of Checker, Simon, and Rosser and lives in northwest Chicago with his wife.

ORDER INFORMATION

To order additional copies of Happy (Freilich) Days Revisited, contact Jack Nusan Porter at jacknusan@earthlink.net or contact:

The Spencer Press
79 Walnut Street, Unit 4
Newtonville, Mass. 02460-1331
(617) 965-8388.

I would like to order:

_____copies for $18.00 each   _____
    plus shipping & handling   _____
                Total   _____

Name: _____

Address: _____

City: _____State: _____ Zip: _____

Telephone: _____

E-mail address: _____

checks or cash only.
$4.00 shipping & handling for the first book $1.00 each additional.
Discounts available

www.ingramcontent.com/pod-product-compliance
Lightning Source LLC
Chambersburg PA
CBHW022154080426
42734CB00006B/434